American City

St. Louis Architecture
Three Centuries of Classic Design

Text by Robert Sharoff
Photographs by William Zbaren

Published in Australia in 2010 by
The Images Publishing Group Pty Ltd
ABN 89 059 734 431
6 Bastow Place, Mulgrave, Victoria 3170, Australia
Tel: +61 3 9561 5544 Fax: +61 3 9561 4860
books@imagespublishing.com
www.imagespublishing.com

National Library of Australia Cataloguing-in-Publication entry:

Author:	Sharoff, Robert.
Title:	American city : St Louis architecture : three centuries of design / by Robert Sharoff ; photography by William Zbaren.
ISBN:	9781864704297 (hbk.)
Series:	American city series.
Notes:	Includes index.
Subjects:	Architecture—Missouri—St Louis.
	Saint Louis (Mo.)—Buildings, structures, etc.
Other Authors/Contributors:	Zbaren, William.
Dewey Number:	720.977866

Coordinating editor: Beth Browne

Designed by Liska + Associates

Pre-publishing services by United Graphic Pte Ltd, Singapore

Printed on 150gsm Quatro Silk Matt by Everbest Printing Co. Ltd., in Hong Kong/China

IMAGES has included on its website a page for special notices in relation to this and its
other publications. Please visit www.imagespublishing.com.

For Mr. and Mrs. St. Louis,
Arthur and Marjorie Zbaren

Acknowledgements

A book of this scope – the first oversized volume on St. Louis architecture since the 1920s – required visionary sponsors who both cherish the city's heritage of outstanding design and are committed to its future growth and success.

The authors would like to thank three remarkable individuals and their companies whose enthusiastic support allowed this project to proceed.

The three are Robert A. Wislow, chairman and chief executive officer of U.S. Equities Realty in Chicago, Robert G. Clark, chairman of Clayco Inc. in St. Louis and Michael F. Neidorff, chairman and chief executive officer of Centene Corporation in the St. Louis suburb of Clayton.

Mr. Neidorff has overseen Centene's outstanding growth since 1996. He, his wife Noemi and Centene are active supporters of many charities and important institutions in the St. Louis area. It was Mr. Neidorff's foresight, vision and passion for excellence, as well as his early engagement of architect Gyo Obata of HOK, that led to the creation of Centene Plaza, the St. Louis area's most architecturally significant new office building. Messrs. Wislow and Clark are real estate developers known for their industry expertise and also for their wide-ranging community and philanthropic endeavors. Mr. Wislow co-founded U.S. Equities in 1978 and has developed numerous architecturally significant buildings in the United States and South America. In the early 2000s, he played an important role in the development of Millennium Park in Chicago, a project that has become a much-studied template for downtown redevelopment and revitalization. Mr. Clark founded Clayco, a real estate construction and development firm, in 1984 and has gone on to build hundreds of buildings in St. Louis and around the country. Among his recent St. Louis projects are Busch Stadium and the Edward A. Doisy Research Center at St. Louis University. Clayco and U.S. Equities, along with The Koman Group, collaborated with Mr. Neidorff and Centene on the design, development and construction of Centene Plaza.

The authors would also like to thank designer Steve Liska of Liska + Associates for his impeccable taste and for his steady hand on the tiller.

The authors would also like to thank Paul Wagman of Fleischman Hilliard for many lunches and a matchless Rolodex; former Landmarks Association of St. Louis Director Carolyn Hewes Toft for sharing her encyclopedic knowledge of the city and its architects; Deputy Mayor for Development Barbara Geisman for smoothing the way (and a great walking tour!); Realtor Joan Wendt for lending us the grooviest penthouse in Clayton; Landmarks Association Director Jefferson Mansell for fact-checking assistance and general good vibes, and Journalist Robert Duffy for intros and support.

The authors would also like to thank John Steffen, who dreamed of Paris on the Mississippi and provided crucial early support and encouragement.

Photographing 50 structures requires gaining access to numerous buildings and vantage points. Sometimes the access is to the structure itself, sometimes to a nearby building. In this regard, the authors would like to thank David Belsky (Isaac H. Lionberger House); Gerald Brooks (St. Louis Public Library); Karen Hagenow (Missouri Botanical Garden Museum and Library); Craig Heller (First Bell Telephone Building); Erin Hentz (Fox Theater); Michael Kelley and Frances Percich (Union Station); Dale Kimberlin (Centene Plaza); Mary Marshall (St. Louis Museum of Art); Anthony Paraino (Anheuser Busch Brew House); Janet Powell (Flight Cage); Jerome Pratter (Merchandise Mart); Emily Rauh Pulitzer (Pulitzer Foundation for the Arts); Kim Singer (Mildred Lane Kemper Museum); Bob Stewart (Grant Medical Clinic); Steven Stogel (Old Post Office); Jim Wilson (Missouri Athletic Club); Gary Tetley, Andy Trivers and Richard Lay (Wainwright Tomb).

Contents

Introduction

Photographer Bill Zbaren and I spent the summer of 2007 living and working in a loft across the street from the Old Post Office in downtown St. Louis. I never got used to it.

Every morning, I would get up, make a cup of coffee, open the blinds of the enormous bay window and be overwhelmed all over again by the view. I used to compare it to having the set from *La Boheme* outside our window.

The Old Post Office is a huge, ornate Second Empire structure built in the years following the Civil War. The façade consists of tiers of classical columns topped by a magnificent mansard roof studded with oculi windows. The gray granite walls are four feet thick. The building has a moat.

Inside, meanwhile, there are elaborate mosaic tile floors, cast-iron columns and staircases, and numerous hand-carved marble fireplaces.

But why was it there? What combination of historical circumstance and architectural inspiration led to the construction of a building that looks like it would be more at home in Belle-Époque Paris than in a 19th-century American river town? (Albeit a river town that was founded by French fur traders and at one time was the fourth largest city in the country …)

We were there to find out.

Back in the early 2000s, Bill and I created the *American City* series as a way to explore and celebrate the amazing historic architecture contained in older cities around the country. There's no shortage of books about the architecture of New York, Chicago or Los Angeles. But the architecture of St. Louis – and, for that matter, Detroit, Cleveland, Milwaukee and numerous other cities – is another story.

The format is the top 50 buildings – not the top 50 Modern buildings or the top 50 Art Deco buildings, but the top 50 of everything right down to public works projects like bridges

and water towers. (St. Louis, by the way, has the most amazing water towers of any American city.) A little hubristic, you say? So be it.

The only ground rules are no ruins and no houses or churches. We have been known to break both of these rules but they are a good place to start.

We began by crisscrossing the city in every direction using guidebooks, history books and recommendations from friends, experts and acquaintances. Then we created a list that ultimately had more than 100 possibilities. The next step was getting the list down to 50. This involved multiple return visits and many late-night discussions about who was inspired by what 150 years ago and whether or not Cass Gilbert might, just possibly, be God.

The final list is a mix of official landmarks such as the Eads Bridge, the Wainwright Building and Union Station and less obvious buildings that nevertheless represent a high level of architectural achievement.

Bill and I think of ourselves as preservationists. More than anything, however, we love that moment when we round a corner in a strange part of town and are stopped dead in our tracks by a masterpiece we had no idea was even there.

Why do we do it? That's why we do it.

Robert Sharoff
William Zbaren

Detail, St. Louis Union Station

St. Louis: Architectural Lives and Legends

1. The Cream of Everything in the World

Even Henry Adams, that most acerbic of 19th-century memoirists, was bowled over by the St. Louis World's Fair.

"The world had never witnessed so marvelous a phantasm," he wrote, before going on to describe "long lines of white palaces, exquisitely lighted by thousands on thousands of electric candles, soft, rich, shadowy, palpable in their sensuous depths … One enjoyed it with iniquitous rapture."

Adams was one of about 20 million visitors to the 1904 Louisiana Purchase Exposition, which celebrated a century of growth in St. Louis. During this period, the city went from being a small fur-trading post on the upper Mississippi River to the nation's fourth largest metropolis.

At a time when Chicago was still a rough settlement of log huts, St. Louis was a bustling city of elegant hotels, theaters and government buildings with a levee district that stretched for several miles along the riverfront and was one of the marvels of 19th-century commerce.

"They boast at St. Louis that they command 46,000 miles of navigable river water," wrote one 19th-century visitor, the British novelist and travel writer Anthony Trollope. "To no city can have been given more means of riches."

These riches were on ample display at the Fair, which sprawled over 1,200 acres of Forest Park, a large tract of rolling land at the city's western boundary.

The Exposition opened on April 30, 1904, with a ceremony that began with President Theodore Roosevelt pressing a telegraph key in the East Room of the White House to ignite the Fair's electrical system.

The highlight was the "Ivory City," a collection of 12 enormous Beaux Arts exhibition halls grouped around a grand basin at the foot of what was called Art Hill. The largest – the Palace of Agriculture – occupied more than 18 acres. There was also a massive, circular Festival Hall that contained a 3,500-seat auditorium.

Except for one – the Palace of Fine Arts – all were temporary structures constructed of plaster and lath. The halls were outlined in tens of thousands of electric light bulbs in the most impressive display of outdoor illumination ever attempted.

Five of the halls were designed by prominent St. Louis architects and firms such as Theodore Link, Eames & Young, and Barnett, Haynes & Barnett. A sixth local architect, Isaac Taylor, served as Director of Works, a position that involved supervising the construction of what is still generally considered to be one of the largest World's Fairs ever held.

The remaining halls were designed by highly regarded East Coast architects and firms such as Cass Gilbert, Carrere & Hastings, and Louis Masqueray. Masqueray, who had previously worked for Carrere & Hastings, Richard Morris Hunt, and Warren & Wetmore, also served as the Fair's Chief of Design.

"The buildings were elegant and formal and were constructed in the approved palatial style," wrote Sally Benson in *Meet Me In St. Louis*, a book and film that even today defines how many people view the city. "There was no thought of dynamic expression or crude force in back of anything … Greek goddesses presided over the domes, classic and beautiful … It was the cream of everything in the world."

Classicism lingered longer in St. Louis than just about anywhere else in the United States. Indeed, almost all of the city's greatest architects were Classicists and it is still the default style of the city, used for everything from downtown skyscrapers to public works projects like parks and bridges.

Along with all of those pillars and pediments, however, is an insistent – at times visionary – streak of Modernism that has

Detail, Eads Bridge

moved the needle of architecture forward on more than one occasion. Three structures in particular stand out in this regard: the Eads Bridge, the Wainwright Building and the Gateway Arch.

It is a legacy well worth celebrating. But in order to understand it, one needs to know how it all began.

2. I Have Found a Situation

St. Louis was founded in 1764 by Pierre Laclede, a French fur trader from New Orleans, who had been granted a trading monopoly for what was then known as the Upper Louisiana Territory. The site was a limestone bluff on the west bank of the Mississippi River just south of the confluence of the Missouri River.

"I have found a situation," Laclede wrote, "where I intend establishing a settlement which in the future shall become one of the most beautiful cities in the world."

The original plan – very similar to New Orleans – consisted of three parallel streets along the river with a total of about two dozen blocks. At the top of the bluff were a few miles of farms and fields that eventually faded into wilderness.

The French lost control of the city to the Spanish in 1770 but regained it in 1800 long enough for the Emperor Napoleon to sell it to the United States as part of the $15 million Louisiana Purchase. In 1804, the French flag was officially replaced by the stars and stripes and the city assumed its historic role as the Gateway to the West.

At that time, St. Louis – a city of about 180 stone and wood houses – had a population of about 1,000 residents.

While none of these buildings still exist, drawings and engravings of the period show that they resembled houses in Quebec and other French colonies with vertical post construction, hipped roofs and expansive verandahs and galleries.

English novelist Charles Dickens left an evocative account of the original village in *American Notes,* a book he published following a six-month tour of the United States in the early 1840s. "In the old French portion of the town," he wrote, "the thoroughfares are narrow and crooked, and some of the houses are very quaint and picturesque: being built of wood, with tumble-down galleries before the windows, approachable by stairs, or rather ladders, from the street. There are queer little barbers' shops and drinking-houses, too, in this quarter; and [an] abundance of crazy old tenements with blinking casements such as may be seen in Flanders."

St. Louis played a leading role in one of the most romanticized periods in American history – the Steamboat Era, lasting roughly from the 1820s to the start of the Civil War. The first steamboat to tie up at the city's wharf was the *Zebulon M. Pike* – named for an early explorer of the Upper Mississippi region – in 1817. By the 1840s, St. Louis was the second busiest port in the west after New Orleans with upwards of 2,000 steamboats a year arriving and departing.

A gauge of business activity during this period can be gleaned from the statistics from the 1849 St. Louis Fire, which began on the morning of May 17 and quickly engulfed about 15 blocks of the riverfront levee district. By the time the fire burned out, about 430 buildings and 23 steamboats had been destroyed with total losses estimated at $6.1 million. The 23 steamboats and their cargoes accounted for $600,000 of that figure.

The steamboat industry kicked off a 40-year period of growth for the city and by 1850 the population had surged to 77,860 residents. During this time, the city began to assume its current dimensions and architects emerged as significant players in the city's development.

3. The Dean of St. Louis Architects

The history of 19th-century St. Louis architecture is bracketed by two epic boondoggles: the Old Courthouse and City Hall.

The former – a handsome Greek Revival structure topped by an iron dome modeled on St. Peter's in Rome – broke ground in 1838 and was not completed until 1862. The latter – a loose adaptation of Paris's city hall, the Hôtel de Ville – took even longer. The project was first proposed in 1868 but city officials did not announce a design competition until 1889 and the building was not completed until 1904.

In both cases, construction waxed and waned over the years, succeeding teams of architects were hired and fired and accusations of profiteering and financial mismanagement proliferated. The miracle is that both buildings are magnificent structures that betray no hint of their intensely troubled gestation periods.

The Old Courthouse involved six different architects – eight, if one includes two early unbuilt designs. One of them was George I. Barnett (1815–1898), an Englishman who is often referred to as the "Dean of St. Louis architects."

Barnett, who was born in Nottingham, England, immigrated to the United States in 1839 after serving an apprenticeship with Sir Thomas Hine, a prominent English architect of the period. Over the course of his nearly 50-year career, Barnett designed hundreds of buildings in a variety of styles with Greek Revival, Italianate and Gothic being the most prominent. His commissions ranged from numerous houses and churches to important civic and commercial projects both in St. Louis and around the state.

More than any other designer, Barnett established Classicism as the city's dominant architectural language. His proportions were unerring, his ornamentation both restrained and dramatic. He also created the city's most enduring architectural dynasty as both his son, Thomas P. Barnett, and grandson, George D. Barnett, followed in his footsteps and became leading architects in their own right.

"He was young at eighty years of age and his ideas were youthful and more optimistic than men I know at thirty," wrote Thomas Barnett after his father's death. "So wrapped up was he in his art and in all things done in the art world that he had no time to grow old or to become bored with the commonplaces of life."

The Missouri Botanical Garden and nearby Tower Grove Park have between them the largest grouping of Barnett structures in the city. These include a museum, two greenhouses, a gate, a gatehouse, a tomb and two houses built for Henry Shaw, the founder of the Garden. These buildings – carefully detailed and in a range of traditional styles – provide an evocative view of the city in its early years.

In 1881, Barnett – by then a revered figure in the city – was honored at a dinner at one of his last major commissions, the Southern Hotel, where he was presented with a gold watch and a silver tea service. Afterwards, he was eulogized by A.J. Conant, a painter renowned for his portraits of local notables.

"You belong to that unbroken line of men who have recorded in solid rock the continuous history of the human race," said Conant, "You have justly earned that enviable reputation which places you in the front rank of the architects of our land."

4. This Is Going to Be My River

The Civil War had a devastating effect on St. Louis and on Missouri, a slave state that nevertheless sided with the North. Slavery had never been much of a factor in St. Louis. Out of a total population of 160,773 in 1860, less than one percent were slaves. Still, the city suffered inordinately as river traffic came to a halt on the lower Mississippi due to various Confederate blockades while trade with the upper Mississippi region was diverted to Chicago.

St. Louis's fabled Levee District never recovered. In his memoir *Life on the Mississippi*, Mark Twain, who began his career as a steamboat pilot, described what he saw during a melancholy visit to the city's waterfront in the early 1880s: "Half a dozen lifeless steamboats, a mile of empty wharves … a wide and soundless vacancy where the serried hosts of commerce used to contend. Here was desolation, indeed … St. Louis is a great and prosperous and advancing city; but the river-edge seems dead past resurrection."

The primary economic drivers of the second half of the 19th century were railroads and St. Louis had some catching up to do. By the late 1860s, eight rail lines converged on the city. Coming and going, however, passengers and freight all had to disembark at the river, transfer to ferry boats and re-board a different train on the opposite shore. By some calculations, shipping a barrel of flour 1,500 feet across the river cost half as much as it did to ship it 1,200 miles upstream from New Orleans.

A bridge had first been proposed in 1839 and rejected due to cost. After the disaster of the war, however, the momentum was irresistible. The man who designed and supervised the construction of what ultimately became the world's first steel truss bridge was James Eads, one of St. Louis's great homegrown geniuses.

Eads (1820–1887) was born in Lawrenceburg, Indiana, a small town just west of Cincinnati on the Ohio River. When he was 13, his family moved to St. Louis where his mother ran a boarding house facing the river. According to one legend, on first seeing the Mississippi, he whispered, "This is going to be my river."

At 22, after working as a clerk on a steamboat, Eads founded an underwater salvage company using a diving bell he had invented and went on to conduct over 500 explorations of the river bottom. During this period, he became probably the foremost expert on the Mississippi's ever-shifting topography and flow.

"Every atom that moves onward in the river," he said, "is controlled by laws as fixed and certain as those which direct the majestic march of the heavenly spheres."

In 1867, Eads proposed that St. Louis construct a massive two-tier bridge – the upper level for foot and carriage traffic, the lower

level for trains – at the foot of Washington Avenue that consisted of three 500-plus-foot steel arches bracketed by masonry approaches on either shore modeled after Roman aqueducts.

The total length was 6,220 feet. The estimated cost – which the city funded by selling stock both locally and in New York – was $4.5 million.

Construction began in 1868 and went on for seven years. In May 1874, 15,000 people paid a nickel apiece to walk across the almost completed span. On July 2, Eads conducted a final test of his creation by rolling 14 locomotives back and forth across the bridge for seven hours. There were no problems.

The official opening on July 4, 1874, attracted over 200,000 people from all over the region and included a 100-gun salute, a 14-mile parade and speeches by Eads as well as by various mayors, governors and senators. "Everything which prudence, judgment and the present state of science could suggest to me and my assistants has been carefully observed …" said Eads. "Every computation … has been made by different individuals thoroughly competent to make them … the possibility of error nowhere exists."

Except, perhaps, in regard to the budget. The final cost was $11 million. And even though the bridge is generally credited with ushering St. Louis into the railroad age, the company that was formed to build and operate it went bankrupt the following year.

5. A Proud and Soaring Thing

The latter decades of the 19th century are often described as St. Louis's Golden Age. The city's population reached 310,000 people in 1870, making it the country's fourth largest metropolis. By 1890, that figure was 451,770.

Fueled by a burgeoning rail network of about two dozen lines that stretched from coast to coast, the city became a leading manufacturing and distribution center specializing in consumer goods such as tobacco, footwear and apparel, furniture, stoves and ranges and building materials. Downtown, the central business district expanded with the development of two vast warehouse districts, Washington Avenue to the north and Cupples Station to the south.

"On every hand," noted *Harper's Weekly* in 1888, "is seen the steady march of improvement in architecture, in streets, in parks ... In the business part of the city the two and three story buildings that so long lined its thoroughfares are passing away and in their places are springing up magnificent structures of stone and iron with all the advantages of the modern metropolitan style of architecture."

The late 1800s were also a watershed moment in American architecture, a time when a booming national economy and advances in building materials and technology led to both new buildings and new kinds of buildings.

There was also a concomitant desire among many architects to move beyond European models and create a uniquely American style of architecture. Three important architects in this regard were Henry Hobson Richardson, Harvey Ellis and Louis Sullivan, all of whom completed major commissions in St. Louis during this period.

Richardson (1838–1886), the great-grandson of scientist Joseph Priestly, was born on a sugar plantation in Louisiana and subsequently attended both Harvard University and the Ecole des Beaux-Arts in Paris. (He was only the second American student – after Richard Morris Hunt – to attend the latter institution.)

Richardson began his practice in New York in 1866 and eight years later moved it to Brookline, Massachusetts. "I'll plan anything a man wants, from a cathedral to a chicken coop," he once said and very nearly did.

Richardson's powerful Romanesque forms and rusticated details had distinct Medieval precedents. Nevertheless, they were widely adopted as templates for modern American churches, railroad stations and government buildings.

In 1885, *American Architect and Building News*, an influential trade journal, published the results of a readership poll on the subject of the 10 finest American buildings. Half the list was devoted to Richardson's projects.

Richardson's most important commissions included Trinity Church in Boston, the Allegheny County Courthouse in Pittsburgh and the Marshall Field Warehouse in Chicago, all of which were widely influential in cities around the country.

In the 1880s, Richardson also designed three houses in St. Louis for members of the wealthy Lionberger family, who were related by marriage to Richardson's chief assistant, St. Louis native George Shepley. (Only one – the Isaac H. Lionberger house – still stands.)

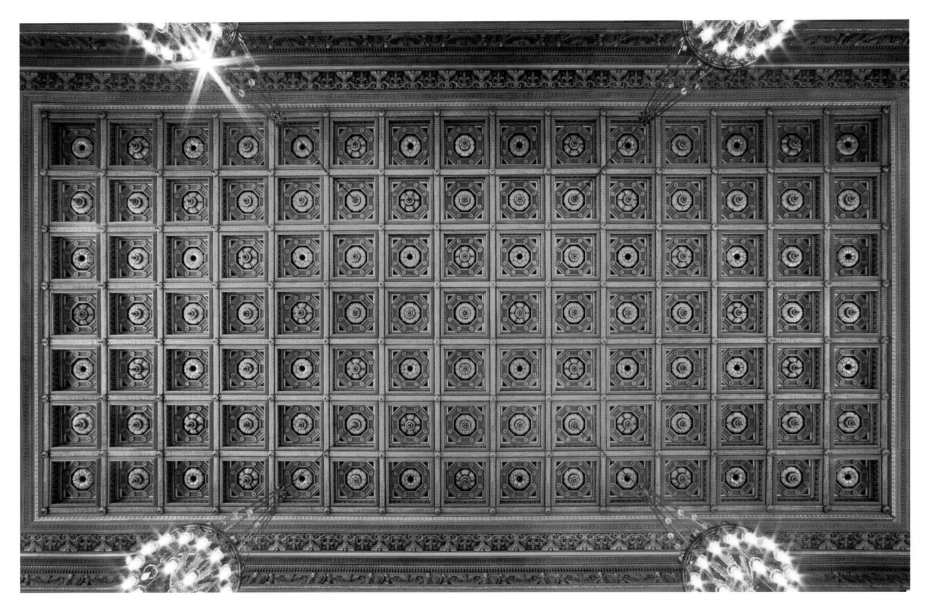

Detail, Delivery Room,
St. Louis Public Library

The houses – and especially Richardson's bold, naturalistic ornamentation – were widely popular in St. Louis, as any visitor to the Central West End neighborhood and the city's other turn-of-the-century residential areas can attest.

Harvey Ellis (1852–1904), on the other hand, labored for most of his life in relative obscurity before the details of his career were pieced together after his death and he was revealed as one of 19th-century America's most interesting designers.

Born in Rochester, New York, to an upstate politician, his exposure to higher education began and ended with a single year at West Point. He worked briefly for Henry Richardson from 1877–78 but spent most of his career drifting between various firms in Rochester, St. Paul, St. Joseph, and St. Louis.

"He was a master of composition" but also "an artist and a romanticist … careless of results and apparently without any marked ambition," said Chicago architect Hugh Garden in a eulogy published in 1908.

Ellis spent the years between 1888 and 1893 in St. Louis where he designed such remarkable structures as St. Louis City Hall, the Compton Hill Water Tower and – his masterpiece – the

Washington Terrace Gate. Like Richardson, his forms were Medieval. His approach, however, was both romantic and picturesque. He was a master of the architectural folie – exquisitely designed structures of a ceremonial or ornamental nature, which he imbued with a lyrical, fairytale quality.

Ellis spent the last two years of his life in Syracuse, New York, designing furniture, textiles and interiors for Gustave Stickley's *Craftsman Magazine*. "The only things he seemed to care for were to paint cryptic, unsalable pictures under a still north light, with plenty of time and plenty of cigarettes," said one friend.

Louis Sullivan (1856–1924), while not the creator of Modernism – there is no one creator – was the movement's guiding theorist with his "form follows function" credo and calls to reject the Classicism of the past in favor of a more organic approach to design. To the degree that he had influences, they tended to be writers and philosophers such as Walt Whitman and Ralph Waldo Emerson rather than architects.

The son of an Irish dancing master in Boston, he attended the Massachusetts Institute of Technology before moving to Chicago in 1873. Several years later, he teamed up with architect Dankmar Adler in the firm of Adler & Sullivan and the pair went on to create such groundbreaking structures as the Auditorium Building in Chicago, the Guaranty Building in Buffalo and the Bayard Building in New York.

They also designed four buildings in St. Louis – two office buildings, a hotel and a tomb – and, in the process, altered the course of architectural history.

In 1890, Sullivan was contacted by Ellis Wainwright, a wealthy brewer who had recently acquired a prime site at the corner of Seventh and Chestnut streets and was looking to erect a speculative office building.

Tall buildings – the term "skyscraper" had not yet been coined – were a relatively new idea then, made possible by advances in steel framing methods and foundation engineering. The problem, however, was that nobody really knew what a tall building should look like.

Sullivan changed all that. "What is the chief characteristic of the tall office building?" he asked. The answer, he believed, was self-evident. "It must be tall. The force and power of altitude must be in it, the glory and pride of exaltation must be in it. It must be every inch a proud and soaring thing …"

The 10-story Wainwright Building, which Sullivan supposedly designed in a matter of minutes, had a profound effect on skyscraper design.

"Until Louis Sullivan showed the way," said Frank Lloyd Wright, who began his career working for Sullivan, "high buildings lacked unity. They were built up in layers. All were fighting height instead of gracefully and honestly accepting it."

"The Wainwright turns out more and more to be the prototype of all contemporary office buildings," noted architect Philip Johnson in the 1980s during the protracted battle to save the building. "In the Wainwright, Sullivan imposed his artistic will on a pile of identical rooms in such a skillful manner that it can still be studied by the practicing architect today."

6. The Promise of Immortal Fame

Richardson, Ellis and Sullivan were only occasional presences in St. Louis – out of town celebrities who dropped in to execute various high-profile commissions. Far more important were the architects who actually lived and worked in the city during this period. Three of the most important were Theodore Link, Isaac Taylor and William Ittner.

Link (1850–1923), who was born in Germany and educated at schools in Heidelberg and Paris, immigrated to St. Louis in 1873, where he found initial employment as a draftsman for the Atlantic & Pacific Railroad. A year later, he became

Detail, Merchandise Mart

Roberts, Johnson & Rand Shoe Company Building. The former, which Link created with his then-partner, Edward Cameron, is modeled after Richardson's Allegheny County Courthouse and was the largest train station in America when it was completed in 1894. The Roberts, Johnson Building, on the other hand, is a more quixotic affair – a melding of Sullivan and George Barnett. The form is the Wainwright Building while the lush ornamentation is a dazzling mix of Classical and Egyptian motifs. More than any other building, it embodied the contradictions and occasional harmonies that roiled the waters of the St. Louis architecture community in the years following the 1904 World's Fair.

Towards the end of his career, Link described the life of an architect as "three quarters drudgery, no play and rarely a reward of full unstinted appreciation." Why did he do it? "The promise of immortal fame."

Isaac Taylor (1850–1917) also did a version of the Wainwright Building – the Bee Hat Building on Washington Avenue – but remained primarily a Classicist, befitting an architect who began his career working for George Barnett.

Taylor, who was born in Nashville and graduated from St. Louis University, joined Barnett's office in 1868 as an apprentice and was eventually named partner. In the early 1880s, he went out on his own.

At his peak, Taylor had one of the largest architectural firms in the city with 10 draftsmen laboring under the supervision of Oscar Enders, his chief designer and renderer. Taylor's commissions ranged from high-profile civic and commercial structures such as the Municipal Courts Building and the Jefferson Memorial to hotels and residences.

It is interesting to compare how Taylor's work was regarded during his lifetime with how it appears today. A satirical profile published in a local magazine in 1906 commented that, "Beauty is not his strong point … His specialty is big, square,

an architectural renderer for Julius Pitzman, an engineer and planner who was then involved in laying out Forest Park.

In 1876, with Pitzman's backing and over the objections of one official who described the 26-year-old Link as "a whippersnapper boy with kid gloves and an effeminate mustache," he was named Superintendent of Public Parks. He lasted two years and then left town for extended stints in Pittsburgh, Philadelphia and New York before returning to St. Louis in 1883 and opening his first architectural office.

Link designed over a hundred buildings during his career with two of the most remarkable being Union Station and the unornamented commercial buildings, like gigantic packing boxes. No gingerbread for him."

Few people today would say that Taylor's buildings lack beauty. The forms may be huge, but Taylor knew exactly what he was doing and the results are surprisingly lyrical and delicate.

His apogee was the 1904 World's Fair, for which he laid out the grounds, reviewed the plans and supervised the construction of the 12 enormous exhibition palaces that made up the "Ivory City." He also designed a number of secondary buildings, including the State of Missouri Building.

His efforts did not go unrecognized. In a history of the Fair published in 1904, the authors noted that, "Director Taylor was in every respect equal to the task and his complete work, if it could have been permanent, would have remained one of the greatest architectural wonders of the world, an achievement overshadowing the fabled labors of Hercules."

The name William Ittner (1864–1936) evokes two things in St. Louis: schools and brickwork. The son of a bricklayer who eventually became a U.S. congressman, Ittner attended both Washington University and Cornell University before beginning his career as an apprentice with Eames & Young, a large downtown architecture firm. He also, briefly, established a partnership with Theodore Link and Alfred Rosenheim.

Ittner's career did not really take off, however, until he was named Commissioner of School Buildings for the St. Louis Board of Education in 1897. He served for 13 years and then became the Board's consulting architect for an additional four years.

During this period, Ittner transformed the public school system in St. Louis by designing and building 50 new school buildings that incorporated his then-radical ideas about educational facilities. Ittner was one of the first architects in the country to propose such amenities as gymnasiums, libraries and auditoriums. He also championed such innovations as E-shaped and L-shaped floorplans to maximize natural light as well as modern ventilation and sanitation systems.

A school's "inviting exterior," he said, should "represent the best, most thoroughly planned structure in the community and its interior the best of all places for work, recreation and study."

Over the course of his long career, Ittner designed about 500 schools for districts around the country while also maintaining an architecture practice in St. Louis that designed a number of prominent downtown commissions.

Throughout his career, brick was his favorite material and the intricate cross-hatched brickwork patterns he designed are a familiar motif in St. Louis.

"Ever seeking for new effects in the blending of colors, Mr. Ittner has obtained a greater variety and elegance of texture in his brick walls than perhaps any living architect," noted the *Architectural Record* in 1925, then and now the publication of record for the architectural field.

7. Exuberant Style

In the years after the World's Fair, St. Louis moved, haltingly, it must be admitted, to embrace the then-new City Beautiful movement. The movement, which began as an outgrowth of the 1893 Chicago World's Fair's "White City," stressed Beaux Arts planning and architectural ideas in pursuit of urban beautification and social harmony. St. Louis, for all of its superb Classical architecture, lacked many basic public amenities such as parks, plazas, sewers and streetlights.

St. Louis "is a very ugly town," said attorney Isaac H. Lionberger – he of the Henry Richardson house – in testimony before the city's plan commission in 1918. He went on to complain that "Westmoreland Place, where I now reside, was twelve years ago a charming, clean and quiet retreat; it is today

Detail, Municipal Courts Building

as unclean atmospherically, and also as noisy, as was my boyhood's residence on (downtown) Chestnut Street in 1860."

The answer was a $84.7 million bond issue – the largest city bond issue in United States history up to that point – that voters approved in 1923. Among other projects, the issue funded new street lights and sewer lines, hospitals, parks, a war memorial and a plaza across from Union Station that was the beginning of the Gateway Mall.

A new, younger group of architects began to emerge during this period. Preston Bradshaw (1880–1949), a Columbia University graduate who worked briefly as a draftsman for McKim, Mead & White in New York, arrived in St. Louis in 1907 and went on to design such local landmarks as the Chase, Mayfair and Coronado hotels as well as the Paul Brown office building in an exuberant style that combined Classical and Moorish elements.

Guy Study (1880–1959), an Indiana native, graduated from Washington University in 1908 and then spent three years studying in Europe before returning to St. Louis where – in association with several different partners – he carved out an interesting career as a designer of houses, churches, schools and civic projects in a variety of historically accurate styles (His 1919 Norman Gothic Church of Our Lady of Lourdes in suburban University City has 3-feet thick solid masonry walls.)

In the teens and 1920s, Study also became a critic and essayist, composing articles and monographs on subjects ranging from the architecture of Washington University and the St. Louis Public Library to the work of fellow St. Louis architect William Ittner.

The firm that dominated the city in those years, however, was Mauran, Russell & Garden, which was founded in 1900 by

John Mauran (1866–1933), Ernest John Russell (1870–1956) and Edward G. Garden (1871–1924.) All three were former employees of Henry Richardson's successor firm, Shepley, Rutan and Coolidge.

The firm – which morphed over time into Mauran, Russell & Crowell – designed many of the largest buildings to be erected in St. Louis during this period, including the Railway Exchange Building, the Federal Reserve Bank, the Southwestern Bell Building and the Stix, Baer & Fuller Department Store. In general, their work was solid and competent but broke no new ground. (For some, of course, this was a damning indictment. In a visit to the city in 1939, Frank Lloyd Wright described the firm's Soldier's Memorial as "a deflowered classic, a Greek thing run through a modernizing mill" and its Federal Courts Building as "a pile of innocuous desuetude.")

8. The Gateway to the West

In the late 1920s and 30s, the issue that increasingly dominated talk of downtown development was the fate of the 37-block riverfront Levee District. By then, river traffic was all but nonexistent and many of the buildings were either vacant or blighted.

In the early 1930s, Luther Ely Smith, a local attorney, enlisted Mayor Bernard Dickmann's support for a plan to replace the district with a riverfront memorial honoring both the Louisiana Purchase and the man who engineered it, President Thomas Jefferson.

They also persuaded President Franklin Roosevelt to sign an executive order in 1935 creating the Jefferson National Expansion Memorial with the National Park Service acting as administrator.

With the sole exception of the Old Cathedral, the entire 90-acre site was leveled in 1939 – hundreds of stores, offices, warehouses and residences dating back to 1818 and representing over a century of St. Louis history. It is a decision that still boggles the minds of preservationists.

"We in the Park Service were supposed to be in the business of saving buildings and here we were pulling them down ..." said Charles Peterson, an architect with the National Park Service who worked on the project. "It was the biggest demolition the Park Service ever had. Nobody had any thought about saving it."

In 1946, the indefatigable Smith raised $225,000 for the largest architectural competition in history for the site. A total of 172 entries were received from such famous names and firms as Walter Gropius, Louis Kahn, Edward Durell Stone, Eliel Saarinen and Skidmore, Owings & Merrill.

Surprising everyone, the winner was Eero Saarinen (1910–1961), Eliel Saarinen's 38-year-old son, who was then at the beginning of his remarkable, if truncated, career. Both Saarinens were based at Cranbrook, a design school and artists colony founded by the elder Saarinen in the 1920s in suburban Detroit.

Eero Saarinen's design team consisted of his wife, sculptor Liliane Saarinen; landscape architect Dan Kiley; designer Alexander Girard, and illustrator J. Henderson Barr. His initial thought was to do a masonry dome a la John Russell Pope's Jefferson Memorial in Washington, D.C. Gradually, however, he devised something far more striking and monumental – a 630-foot-tall stainless steel catenary arch.

Early on, Saarinen explored the idea of having the arch straddle the Mississippi but rejected it on the grounds that "There seemed to be enough bridges, and placing a symbolic bridge between two useful bridges didn't seem right ... Then we came back to the thought that placing it on the west bank was not bad at all. It seemed like sort of a modern adaptation of a Roman triumphal arch ... More and more, it began to dawn on us that the arch was really a gateway ... Gradually, we named it the 'Gateway to the West.'"

Many years later, Susan Saarinen, Eero Saarinen's daughter, recalled the marathon four-month design process that resulted in the Gateway Arch.

"We had chains hanging in our basement so that (my father) could study the proportions of a catenary curve," she said. "There was a huge full-scale model of the stairs for the arch, so that he could be certain that (the) treads ... would be walkable. There was a tramcar model at the office. Eero had everyone, including visitors, climb in and out, and he timed them with a stopwatch to estimate how many people the tram cars could carry in an hour."

Saarinen, said Dan Kiley, "Was a very tough taskmaster. And the people who worked for him really had to be very dedicated to take it ... He thought of nothing else. He never listened to music, he had no activities. He was a fierce competitor, very fierce, even with his father. And he would go to every length to make sure that he was going to win."

Construction began in 1959 after a decade of laborious fundraising and was not completed until 1965. The final cost was about $16.5 million.

The Arch confounded the less-is-more architectural establishment of the period and enchanted everyone else. In 1976, the St. Louis Art Museum commissioned photographer Joel Meyerowitz to produce a documentary portrait of the city. He found himself particularly mesmerized by the Arch.

"There were days when, standing beneath it, I felt I knew the power of the pyramids," he said. "It was restorative, contemplative. It was more than a technological marvel or symbol. It was pure form, the beauty of mathematics, a drawing on the heavens, perfect pitch. I became in awe of it."

Tragically, Eero Saarinen did not live to see the completion of his design. He died in 1961 of a brain tumor at the age of 51.

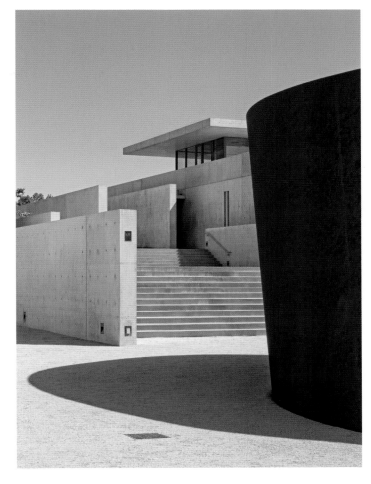

Detail, Pulitzer Foundation for the Arts

9. The Golden Age of Modern Design

The Arch sparked a decade of growth and also signaled the arrival of Modernism as an architectural style in the city. "In striding into its third century," wrote *Time* magazine in an article on the Arch in 1965, "St. Louis is demonstrating how powerful a stimulant to a city's pride both art and architecture can become." Over the next decade, over half a billion dollars of new development would transform the downtown area.

The city's most important early Modernist was Harris Armstrong (1899–1973), a native of Edwardsville, Illinois, whose tobacco salesman father moved the family to suburban St. Louis when Armstrong was a teenager.

Like James Eads and a number of the city's other 19th-century luminaries – but unlike most 20th-century architects – Armstrong was lightly schooled. A high school dropout, he went on to complete a year at Ohio State University in the early 1920s and a few night courses at Washington University while he was working as a draftsman for various downtown firms.

Armstrong did not receive his architectural license until 1942, well after he had established a reputation for innovative design with the 1935 Shanley Building in suburban Clayton, and the 1938 Grant Clinic in the city's Central West End neighborhood. The former, a low-slung International Style medical office with concrete stucco walls and a flat roof, won a silver medal at the 1937 Paris World's Fair.

The latter, a brick medical office with wide overhangs and large windows that recalls both Frank Lloyd Wright and Eliel Saarinen, was intimately scaled and beautifully detailed, traditionally a winning combination in St. Louis. Both buildings are considered among the most important early Modern structures in the city.

Armstrong's most important commission, however, was the 1946 Magic Chef Building, a six-story office building for a manufacturer of stoves and ranges that featured the first glass curtain wall in St. Louis, if not the Midwest. Inside, meanwhile, was a spectacular lobby with a ceiling designed by sculptor Isamu Noguchi. (The building's curtain wall and lobby have been altered by subsequent tenants.)

Modernism took a wavering, quirky course in St. Louis. Minimalism, functionalism, less-is-more – all were tough sells in a city whose architectural DNA remained George Barnett's Classicism. In general, the Modern architects who succeeded in St. Louis were those who chose to embrace rather than challenge its Classical heritage by adhering to certain norms in terms of scale, materials and detailing.

The architects who seemed to grasp this most intuitively were a trio of Japanese designers – Minoru Yamasaki, Fumihiko Maki and Gyo Obata – whose work in the 1950s and 60s ushered in a mini golden age of Modern design for the city.

Minoru Yamasaki (1912–1986), the son of Japanese immigrants in Seattle, attended the University of Washington before starting his career by working for industrial designers George Nelson and Raymond Loewy. In the early 1950s, he teamed up with architects George Hellmuth and Joseph Leinweber in a firm that had dual offices in Detroit and St. Louis. During this period, he designed several major projects for St. Louis, the most notable of which was a new main terminal for Lambert Field, the city's airport.

The terminal – which consisted of three vaulted halls constructed of thin-shell concrete that suggested a streamlined version of one of Classicism's most durable models, the Baths of Caracalla – was the first airport in the country to capture something of the grandeur and elegance so characteristic of 19th-century railroad stations. Much praised when it opened, it remains in use today.

(Less happily, Yamasaki also designed the Pruitt-Igoe Homes, a misguided public housing project located northwest of downtown that ultimately became a nationwide symbol of urban decay and the failure of Modern architecture to address it. In 1972, Pruitt-Igoe, by then a half empty, crime-ridden no man's land, was demolished, the first of many subsequent demolitions across the country.)

Fumihiko Maki (1928–) was born in Tokyo and moved to the United States in the early 1950s to pursue graduate work at Cranbrook and Harvard University's Graduate School of Design. In 1956, he accepted an offer to become a design instructor at Washington University's school of architecture, a position he held until 1962.

Maki's initial reactions to St. Louis were mixed. The city, he says, boasted "many excellent (neoclassical) buildings constructed from the nineteenth century to the early twentieth century" but "very few works of modern architecture that might attract visitors from outside the region."

He also noticed more ominous signs. "The development of (the city's) suburban districts had come at a price," he says. "The downtown area and the old residential districts immediately around it were suffering a decline that was palpable …"

Still, St. Louis provided Maki with a unique opportunity: his first major commission. That building was Steinberg Hall, a two-story masonry building containing offices, classrooms, a library and an auditorium for the university's art and architecture departments. Steinberg has an innovative "folded plate" roof and ceiling that – like William Ittner's brickwork patterns – subsequently became a much-imitated feature in the city.

In the early 1960s, Maki left St. Louis and returned to Tokyo where he became a founding member of the Metabolist Movement, an offshoot of Modernism that stressed organic, fungible design, and one of Japan's most honored architects. In 1993, he won the Pritzker Prize, generally considered architecture's highest award.

In 2006, Maki returned to St. Louis to design an addition to Steinberg Hall – the new Mildred Lane Kemper Art Museum and Walker Hall just north of the original building. His feelings about the city, however, remained ambivalent.

"I sometimes dream of foreign cities, but oddly enough never of Paris or New York," he says. "The city that appears most often in my dreams is St. Louis, and the scene is never of a place I lived in or at Washington University, but of the desolate midtown (area) or some fantastic townscape born of my memory of that place."

Both Yamasaki and Fumihiko Maki had relatively brief exposures to the city. Gyo Obata's influence, however, has been far more profound and lasting. He is, in fact, what George Barnett was in the 19th century: the leading architect of his time.

During the half-century-plus he has lived and worked in St. Louis, Obata (1923–) has reshaped the city both by designing

Detail, Fox Theater

professor – he avoided internment during the Second World War by enrolling as an architecture student at Washington University.

"The day before my family was evacuated to a relocation center," he says, "I was able to leave the West Coast for St. Louis. Many years later, I found out that the chancellor of Washington University went to the Architecture School and asked the students if they would accept me. Fortunately, they agreed."

After graduating in 1945, he went on to get a master's degree from Cranbrook. During this period, he worked briefly for Harris Armstrong and – after graduation – for Skidmore, Owings & Merrill in Chicago. In 1950, he joined Minoru Yamasaki's firm – Hellmuth, Yamasaki & Leinweber – and began working on Lambert Field.

In 1955, Yamasaki resigned and Obata, George Hellmuth and a third colleague, George Kassabaum, reorganized the firm as Hellmuth Obata & Kassabaum – or HOK, as it came to be known.

Obata was one of the first people to realize that architecture in the late 20th century was becoming a far more corporate and collaborative enterprise.

"Architecture itself is becoming big business," he noted in 1967. "The architect today is sort of a catalyst who brings together sociologists, psychologists, personnel managers and others into a type of operations research team responsible for producing a building that will best serve its intended purpose."

Today, with 1,800 employees in 23 offices around the world, HOK is a global force.

Obata's work has evolved considerably over the years. He began as something of a miniaturist and experimentalist with projects such as the American Zinc building and the MacDonnell Planetarium but has gone on to do numerous gigantic skyscrapers. These include Metropolitan Square,

literally hundreds of buildings and restoration projects and by weighing in on numerous civic planning initiatives. He has also played a leading role in creating what is not only the largest architecture firm in the city but also one of the largest in the world.

Obata's introduction to St. Louis came at a propitious moment. The son of Japanese immigrants in San Francisco – his father was a painter as well as a University of California art

One AT&T Center, the Thomas F. Eagleton Courthouse in downtown St. Louis and – most recently – Centene Plaza in suburban Clayton.

10. A City that Believes in Beauty

Like many American cities, St. Louis endured a substantial period of decline in the waning decades of the 20th century. After reaching a peak of 857,000 residents in the 1950s, the population dropped precipitously before bottoming out in the 1990s and early 2000s at around 348,000. (It has since risen to 357,000, making St. Louis the 52nd largest city in the United States.) In a visit to the city in the mid-1960s, architecture critic Ada Louise Huxtable noted that, "All the stages of decay, death, rebirth and rebuilding are currently visible – with the usual successes and failures, ironies and anachronisms."

Ever so slowly, however, a turnaround began, signaled initially by several high-profile preservation campaigns in the early 1970s and 80s. The most significant campaign – which attracted national attention – was for Louis Sullivan's 1892 Wainwright Building, which was scheduled for demolition until a group of concerned citizens began a grassroots campaign to save it. Campaigns for the Old Post Office, Union Station and other landmarks followed. The preservation impulse has remained strong in St. Louis, the most recent example being the revitalization of Washington Avenue, formerly the city's commercial heart and now reborn as a residential loft district.

The city has also continued to attract top-flight architectural and design talent with new buildings, parks and plazas by designers such as Tadao Ando, Maya Lin and Liam Gillick. Downtown, a new stadium for the St. Louis Cardinals baseball team as well as a new sculpture park were recently unveiled. In addition, ambitious plans for renovating the area around the Gateway Arch are currently being discussed.

Sally Benson need not have worried about her hometown succumbing to "dynamic expression" or "crude force."

Midway through its third century, St. Louis remains what it always has been – a bastion of Classicism enlivened by the occasional Modern addition. One of the most charming things about the city is that the 19th century never seems that far away. The ghosts of its great turn-of-the-century artists and architects hover around parks and squares, downtown blocks and residential rows.

There is no shortage of masterpieces. People still marvel over the Old Courthouse, Eads Bridge, Alfred Mullet's Old Post Office, Theodore Link's Union Station, Louis Sullivan's Wainwright Building and many others. St. Louis children still climb the well-worn stone steps of William Ittner's glorious public school buildings.

What is fascinating, ultimately, about St. Louis architecture is the variety of expression and the ongoing appetite for color and detail. This is a city that still believes in beauty as opposed to functionalism.

St. Louis has always been a crossroads, a launching pad for adventurers and entrepreneurs. Looking at the histories of its greatest artists and architects, one is struck by how many were migrants from other cities and countries. They came, as migrants always do, for a better life and the opportunity to do great work.

One such migrant, Minoru Yamasaki, the designer of Lambert Field, once said that, "No matter how good he may be, an architect is still to a great extent controlled by the attitudes and conceptions of the clients, people and society that surround him. If these elements lack the proper imagination and foresight, our environment will not attain the heights that are possible."

In St. Louis, as the buildings clearly show, nothing is impossible.

American City

St. Louis Architecture
Three Centuries of Classic Design

OLD COURTHOUSE

Broadway and Chestnut, Market and Fourth streets
Henry Singleton; George I. Barnett; William Twombley; Barnett, Brewster & Hart; Robert Mitchell; William Rumbold
1839–1864

The Old Courthouse – a cross-shaped Greek Revival structure topped by an iron Italian Renaissance dome – is located on a block the city originally used for stocks, whippings and other forms of public justice. The highlight is the dome, which was designed by William Rumbold and features three tiers of galleries ringed with columns and pilasters along with four majestic lunettes by artist Carl Wimar that depict the founding of St. Louis by Pierre Laclede, DeSoto's discovery of the Mississippi River, a 1789 Indian attack on the village and a puzzling scene of buffalo grazing in Colorado's Cochetopa Pass. (The explanation for the latter is that the Pass represented a possible southern route for the transcontinental railroad that St. Louis business interests were very much in favor of as it included a stop in the city. The railroad's planners, however, ultimately chose a different route.) The $1.2 million courthouse was the most impressive public building west of the Mississippi and a major early tourist attraction. The Old Courthouse was replaced in 1930 by the Civil Courts Building and came close to being demolished as part of the Jefferson Memorial Expansion but was ultimately rescued. Today, the building is a museum and National Historic Monument.

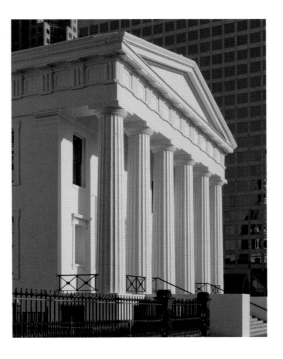

Far Left: The Old Courthouse's dome rises 230 feet and includes four lunettes by artist Carl Wimar

Left: Turtles, catfish and other wildlife native to the Mississippi River are common design motifs in St. Louis as in this decorative iron fence

Top: The Old Courthouse's east portico

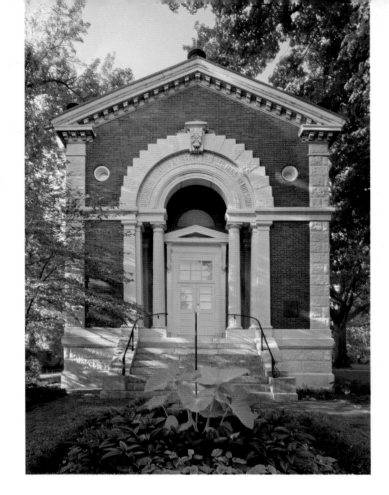

MISSOURI BOTANICAL GARDEN MUSEUM AND LIBRARY

4344 Shaw Boulevard
George I. Barnett
1860

Built to house a collection of botanical books as well as the 60,000 dried plant specimens that Henry Shaw, the founder of the Missouri Botanical Garden, had recently acquired from the estate of German botanist Johann Bernhardi, this stately Georgian Classical structure – which cost $25,000 to construct – was one of the first buildings to be completed in the garden. "I intend to have everything substantial and elegant but on a small scale," said Shaw of his architectural plans. (Too small, according to Shaw's friend and mentor Dr. George Engelmann, who commented that, "there is no working room in the whole business if it be not the basement.") The skylit ceiling features lush floral paintings by Leon Pomarede, a French itinerant artist who traveled between St. Louis and New Orleans painting everything from theater scenery and advertising signs to portraits and landscapes.

GRAND AVENUE WATER TOWER

Grand Boulevard and 20th Street
George I. Barnett
1871

The oldest of St. Louis's three historic water towers, the Grand Avenue Water Tower consists of an octagonal stone base, a 116-foot brick shaft and a cast-iron Corinthian capital. Its total height is 154 feet. The walls of the shaft are about two feet thick at the base and narrow to a foot thick at the top. Inside, an iron standpipe five feet in diameter helped stabilize water pressure in the area. A staircase winds around the pipe leading to the roof. The tower – which cost $45,000 to build – was removed from service in 1912 but remains one of the city's more confounding sights.

EADS BRIDGE

Washington Avenue and the Mississippi River
James Eads
1874

The Eads Bridge was the 19th-century equivalent of the Gateway Arch – a stupendous engineering accomplishment that redefined the city. There are several major "firsts" associated with the structure – it was the world's first steel truss bridge and building it involved the first use of a pneumatic caisson in the United States. (James Eads played up the publicity value of the latter innovation by installing a telegraph terminal in it that allowed workers to communicate with their bosses on the surface and Eads to send greetings to his stockholders in New York.) The three supremely graceful steel spans were fabricated by Andrew Carnegie's Keystone Bridge Company in Pittsburgh over the objections of various experts who questioned the safety of Eads's design. Eads's response: "Must we admit that because a thing never has been done, it never can be, when our knowledge and judgment assure us that it is entirely practicable?" The middle span is 520 feet while the two flanking spans are 502 feet. The total length – including the long approach on the Illinois side – is 6,220 feet. The bridge – the first across the Mississippi at St. Louis – marked the end of the Steamboat Era and hastened the decline of the Levee District while at the same time establishing the city as a major rail hub. The Interstate highway system bypassed the Eads in the 1950s and 60s and the last train went across in 1974. Today, it serves mainly as a vehicular connection to East St. Louis.

RAEDER PLACE

721 North First Street
Frederick William Raeder
1874

This building – as well as a handful of surrounding structures – is all that is left of St. Louis's legendary Levee District, at one time the largest cast iron architecture neighborhood west of New York's SoHo. (The Levee District was demolished in the late 1930s to make way for the Gateway Arch.) Pre-fabricated cast-iron façades and building ornament were ubiquitous in the middle years of the 19th century, available by catalog and (relatively) easy to install. Classical motifs in particular translated well to iron, making it a natural choice for St. Louis. The building – a typical industrial structure of the period – was built as a factory for the Christian Peper Tobacco Co. and renamed Raeder Place in the late 1970s after its original architect, Frederick Raeder. German-born Raeder, who immigrated to the United States in the 1850s, had a long career in St. Louis as a designer of factories, breweries and other industrial buildings.

LINNEAN HOUSE

Missouri Botanical Garden
4344 Shaw Boulevard
George I. Barnett
1882

The Linnean House – named for Carl Linneaus, the pioneering 18th-century Swedish botanist – is the oldest continuously operating greenhouse west of the Mississippi River. In form, the structure recalls the 1761 Orangerie at England's Kew Gardens. The intricately patterned brick walls, however, are pure St. Louis. The entrance is adorned with busts of Linneaus as well as of Asa Gray and Thomas Nuttall by St. Louis sculptor Howard Kretchmar. Gray, an author and professor at Harvard University, was the most prominent American botanist of the 19th century while Nuttall was a British botanist and zoologist who explored the Upper Mississippi and Missouri rivers in the early 1800s. Built to house palms, tree ferns and citrus trees, it now holds the Garden's camellia collection.

OLD POST OFFICE

Olive, Locust, Eighth and Ninth streets
Alfred B. Mullett
1884

Restorations by Patty, Berkabile, Nelson and Harry Weese
& Associates in 1982 and Trivers Associates in 2006

The Old Post Office is one of a handful of flamboyant French
Second Empire public buildings designed by Alfred B. Mullet
in cities around the country while he was Architect of the
U.S. Treasury from 1866 to 1874. (The Old Post Office and the
Old Executive Office Building in Washington, D.C. are the
only two that survive.) The façade consists of stacked tiers of
Doric, Ionic and Corinthian columns topped by a dramatic
mansard roof punctuated with oculi windows and a sculptural
grouping over the front pavilion depicting "Peace and
Vigilance." (The grouping was noted sculptor Daniel Chester
French's first major commission.) Inside, there are mosaic tile
floors, cast-iron columns and staircases as well as numerous
hand-carved Italian marble fireplaces. The total cost was
$6 million. Mullet's opulent taste eventually got the better
of him. In 1874, he was forced to resign his position over
charges of over-spending and financial mismanagement. The
building has narrowly escaped more than one appointment
with the wrecking ball. ("I was shocked to hear that after
all that has been said and done, there is still a chance that the
Old Post Office will be destroyed. What kind of idiocy is
this?" wrote designer – and St. Louis native – Charles Eames
in a scorching letter to the *St. Louis Post Dispatch* in 1965.)
A major renovation in the early 1980s created an atrium
highlighted by a new cast-iron staircase in the center of the
building. A second restoration was completed in 2006. Today,
the building is occupied by a variety of civic and private
businesses and offices.

Left: The 1982 restoration included
creating an atrium in the center of
the building and moving Daniel
Chester French's age-deterioriated
"Peace and Vigilance" sculptural
grouping indoors

Far Left: The Old Post Office's magnificent mansard roof is adorned with a copy of Daniel Chester French's "Peace and Vigilance" sculptural grouping. The original is inside

Left: The building features numerous cast-iron columns

Top: The façade consists of stacked tiers of Doric, Ionic and Corinthian columns

ISAAC H. LIONBERGER HOUSE

3630 Grandel Square
Henry Hobson Richardson
1886

In the year before he died, Boston architect Henry Hobson Richardson designed three houses for members of the wealthy Lionberger family in St. Louis, who were related by marriage to Richardson's chief assistant, George Shepley. This house, which was built as a wedding gift to attorney Isaac Lionberger by his father, John Lionberger, is the only residence that survives. The original house consisted of the entrance and the two left bays. A sympathetic addition was added in 1894 by Richardson's successor firm, Shepley, Rutan & Coolidge. The house and its addition are surprisingly close to Richardson's much-praised Glessner House in Chicago, which was designed during the same period.

MERCHANDISE MART

1000 Washington Avenue
Isaac Taylor
1888

In the years after the completion of the Eads Bridge, Washington Avenue took off as the center of St. Louis's booming wholesale industry. The Merchandise Mart – originally a warehouse for the Liggett & Myers tobacco company – is one of a number of imposing structures that make the street one of the best-preserved 19th-century commercial districts in the country. Architect Isaac Taylor is mainly known for his Classical work, but for this commission he seems to be channeling two proto-Modern structures in Chicago: Henry Richardson's Marshall Field Warehouse and Louis Sullivan's Auditorium Building. It's a massive building – 500,000 square feet – but surprisingly light on its feet. This is due primarily to the broad expanses of glass and the delicacy of the terra cotta ornamentation. In the 1950s, the structure was renamed the Merchandise Mart. In the early 2000s, it was converted to residential apartments.

BELL TELEPHONE BUILDING

920 Olive Street
Shepley, Rutan & Coolidge
1891

An evocative oddity by architect Henry Richardson's successor firm, the Bell Telephone Building is an ambitious attempt to translate Richardson's ideas about form and structure to the skyscraper age. Richardson himself made several attempts in this direction, most notably with the 1876 Hayden Building in Boston, which the Bell building resembles. For a seven-story structure, the Bell is surprisingly massive and imposing with rusticated details that outline the different levels and functions, while at the same time reinforcing the idea of verticality. When it opened, the building's sixth floor housed every telephone operator in St. Louis. The seventh floor, with its Italian renaissance cornice, was added in 1919.

ANHEUSER–BUSCH BREW HOUSE

Bounded by Lynch, South Broadway, Arsenal and I-55
Widman, Walsh & Boisselier
1892

The Brew House – a six-story German Romanesque pile topped by a clock tower – is the highlight of this 142-acre historic brewery complex just south of downtown. Inside is a remarkable skylit atrium surrounded by cast-iron columns and balustrades with additional illumination provided by several iron chandeliers rendered in the form of hop vines. Annual production when the facility opened was about 1.8 million barrels. Today, that number is 15.8 million barrels.

WAINWRIGHT BUILDING

709 Chestnut Street
Adler & Sullivan
1892

Restoration and additions by Mitchell & Giurgola and Hastings & Chivetta in 1981

In 1890, brewer Ellis Wainwright commissioned the Chicago firm of Adler & Sullivan to design a new 10-story office building in downtown St. Louis and the resulting structure changed architecture forever. Skyscrapers were a new idea in the late 1800s, made possible by the introduction of metal framing and advances in foundation engineering. But no one really knew what a skyscraper should look like. Architect Louis Sullivan supplied the answer: "It must be every inch a proud and soaring thing, rising in sheer exultation … from bottom to top … without a single dissenting line." The building – which Sullivan supposedly sketched out in a matter of minutes – cost $561,255 to construct. The ground floor contained spaces for nine stores while the upper floors consisted of about 200 offices plus washrooms and a skylit barbershop on the top floor.

Far Left: The ornamentation of the recessed spandrels varies by floor

Left: The Wainwright's surprisingly understated main entrance features bands of original terra cotta ornamentation

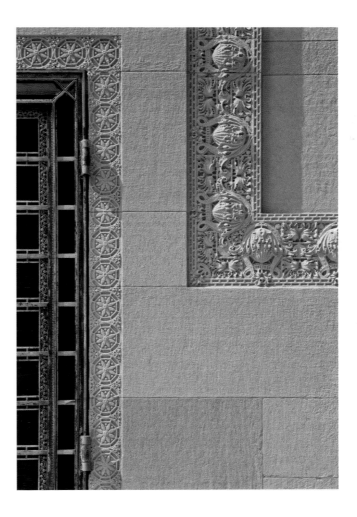

WAINWRIGHT TOMB

Bellefontaine Cemetery
Adler & Sullivan
1892

One of three mausoleums Louis Sullivan designed in his
lifetime (the other two are in Chicago), the Wainwright Tomb
is generally considered one of his most sublime creations.
Architecture critic Ada Louise Huxtable has compared it to the
work of Michelangelo. The building is a memorial to Charlotte
Dickson Wainwright, the young wife of developer Ellis
Wainwright, who died in 1891. Ellis Wainwright, who never
remarried and who died in 1924, is also interred here.
A flawlessly proportioned limestone cube outlined in bands of
delicate ornament and topped by a low dome, it is both serene
and consoling. Inside, a gold star surrounded by angels in the
center of the dome shines down on the side-by-side burial slabs.

33

Top: All four sides of the Wainwright
tomb feature original ornamentation

Right: The tomb's rarely
photographed interior

ST. LOUIS UNION STATION

Market Street between 18th and 20th Streets
Theodore Link and Edward Cameron
Train Shed by George H. Pegram
1894

Restoration by Hellmuth, Obata & Kassabaum in 1985

The station – which cost $6.5 million to construct – is modeled after Henry Richardson's 1884 Allegheny County Courthouse in Pittsburgh. (Richardson's inspiration was the Medieval walled city of Carcassonne.) The structure achieves its own level of distinction, however, by the efficiency of its layout and the sheer beauty of its materials and appointments. The limestone exterior includes a 230-foot clock tower as well as an 11-acre steel train shed that at one time housed 42 tracks. When Union Station opened, it was – by some measurements – the largest rail terminal in the world. Inside, the highlight is the main waiting room, a six-story barrel-vaulted space with numerous stained glass windows and elaborate tile and plasterwork that was designed by Louis Millet, a Chicago designer and stained glass artist who worked extensively with Louis Sullivan and was also the chief decorative painter for the 1904 World's Fair. The station's peak year was 1943 when 71,621 trains carrying 22 million passengers either arrived or departed. Abandoned by Amtrak in 1978, it was sold to a developer in 1985 for $5 million – $1.5 million less than it cost to build – and redeveloped as a popular shopping and tourist destination.

Far Left: Union Station's barrel-vaulted main waiting room

Left (top and middle): The main waiting room's bold ornamentation was designed by Louis Millet, a Chicago artist who worked extensively with architect Louis Sullivan

Left (bottom): The stained glass window over the main entrance symbolizes three important railroad terminals: San Francisco, St. Louis and New York

WASHINGTON TERRACE ENTRANCE GATE

Washington Terrace and Union Boulevard
Harvey Ellis
1894

An unusual feature of residential life in St. Louis is the city's many private streets or "places," most of which were laid out in the late 19th century by city surveyor and land planner Julius Pitzman. These streets – predecessors of today's gated communities – are owned and maintained by their residents and usually have stringent deed restrictions that reinforce the street's economic and architectural consistency. Most also have elaborate gates that both limit access and serve as bulwarks of social status. This exquisite example by one of the city's most enigmatic designers – an adaptation of a 15th-century portal in the German walled city of Lubeck – is the entrance to one such street.

BEE HAT BUILDING

1025 Washington Avenue
Isaac Taylor
1899

Originally the 11th Street Realty Company Building, this loft building was occupied by two different footwear companies in its early days and from 1944 to 2000 by the Bee Hat Company. In 2005, it was renovated into residential apartments. The building is elegantly detailed with delicate arched bays and a cornice of bare-breasted caryatids that recall such Louis Sullivan structures as the Wainwright Building in St. Louis and the Bayard Building in New York. A series of 11 terra cotta lion heads at street level were originally used as downspouts for the building's gutter system but have now been reconfigured as decorative steam valves.

CHEMICAL BUILDING

Northeast corner of Olive and Eighth Streets
Henry Ives Cobb
1896

St. Louis in the late 19th century tended to look east to New York and Boston rather than north to Chicago for imported architectural talent. The exceptions were Louis Sullivan and Henry Ives Cobb, both of whom excelled at color and ornamentation, two things that never go out of style in St. Louis. The 17-story Chemical Building — which recalls Holabird & Roche's now-vanished Tacoma Building in Chicago — was built to serve as offices for the Chemical National Bank but was never used for that purpose. The building has some of the most extravagant cast-iron ornamentation in the city as well as an unusual orieled façade. One gets a sense of the often-uneasy relationship that existed between St. Louis and Chicago by the words of one local critic who described the building as being in "the degenerate Chicago style." In 1903, the firm Mauran, Russell & Garden completed an extensive addition along Eighth Street. The addition, while seamless, destroyed the original and superior proportions.

Far Left, Left and Top: The Chemical Building features some of the most extravagant terra cotta and cast-iron ornamentation in the city

COMPTON HILL
WATER TOWER

Reservoir Park on South Grand between Russell and I-44
Harvey Ellis
1899

Built to control water pressure in the residential area surrounding Tower Grove Park, this is the last of St. Louis's three Victorian-era water towers. (The other two – the Grand Avenue Water Tower and the Bissell Street Water Tower – are on the city's north side.) The exquisitely detailed 179-foot French Romanesque tower was retired from service in 1929. This was the gifted Harvey Ellis's final work in St. Louis.

ST. LOUIS UNIVERSITY MUSEUM OF ART

3663 Lindell Boulevard
Friedlander & Dillon with Lawrence Ewald
1899

This exuberant French Renaissance chateau started off as the home of the exclusive St. Louis Club and included a third-floor ballroom as well as a swimming pool and bowling alley in the basement. In 1925, a fire gutted most of the interior and the structure was rebuilt as offices for the F.W. Woolworth Co. dime store chain. In the 1980s, it was converted first to classrooms and then to a museum for St. Louis University.

FLIGHT CAGE

Forest Park
Architect Unknown
1904

At 228 feet long, 84 feet wide and 50 feet high, the Flight Cage remains one of the largest aviaries in the world. Built at a cost of $17,500 for the 1904 World's Fair by the Smithsonian Institution, it was sold to the city for $3,500 within days of the Exposition's closing and became the founding exhibit for the St. Louis Zoo. The price did not include the birds, however, so the city later paid $7.50 for a pair of Mandarin ducks and $20 for four Canadian geese. In addition, several owls were donated by local residents.

ST. LOUIS ART MUSEUM

Forest Park
Cass Gilbert
1904

Additions and renovations by Louis LaBeaume;
Murphy & Mackey; Hardy, Holzman & Pfeiffer;
Moore Ruble Udell and Smith & Entzeroth

Built as the Fine Arts Pavilion for the 1904 World's Fair, this
magnificent palace subsequently became home to the city's
municipal art museum. (The museum and the nearby St. Louis
Zoo Flight Cage are the only remaining structures from
the fair in Forest Park.) New York architect Cass Gilbert, the
designer of such landmarks as the Woolworth Building
in Manhattan and the United States Supreme Court Building in
Washington, D.C., was one of the country's leading Classicists
and known for his lush detailing and interiors. "A white
marble building is always a source of pride in a community
and it would be very fine to see it up there on the hill among
the trees after the exposition is over," he wrote in his proposal
for the project (He was right about the effect but not the
material. For unexplained reasons, the building was constructed
of limestone.) The Museum's portico features a series of six
sculptures representing what Gilbert believed to be the six most
important eras in art: Egyptian, Classic, Gothic, Renaissance,
Oriental and Modern.

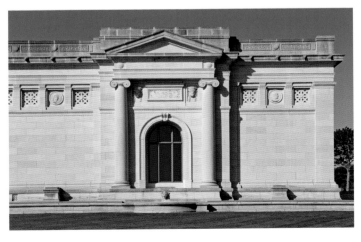

Left: The Art Museum's portico features sculptures symbolizing Egyptian, Classic, Gothic, Renaissance, Oriental and Modern art

Top: The building's roofline is adorned with lion's heads, a common architectural motif in St. Louis

57

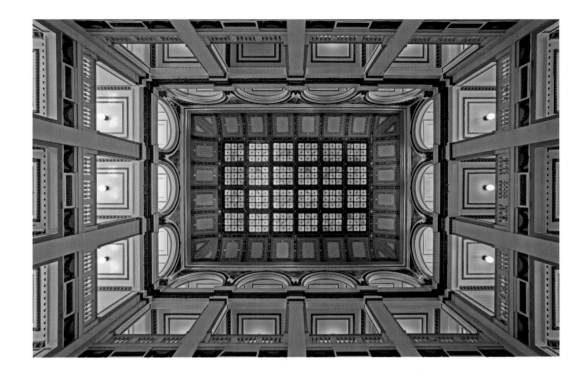

ST. LOUIS CITY HALL

Market Street at Tucker Boulevard
Eckel & Mann with Harvey Ellis
Interior court by Albert Groves
1890–1904

Civic boosters in the late 1800s often described St. Louis as "Paris on the Mississippi," so it is probably not surprising that when the city staged an architectural competition for a new city hall in 1889, the submission that found favor was this adaptation of Paris's city hall, the 17th-century Hôtel de Ville. The hand of Harvey Ellis is evident in the building's many picturesque details. The white marble rotunda by Albert Groves belongs to another era entirely but is equally impressive. Plagued by political interference, construction dragged on for 14 years. The final cost was $1.7 million. The building contains 150 rooms with the most impressive being the Mayor's Office as well as the chambers used by the Board of Aldermen and the Board of Public Service. All are outfitted with murals, elaborate ceilings and decorative details. The rotunda's gold glass skylight is another highlight. The building originally had an 80-foot central bell tower flanked by two smaller towers that were removed in 1936. The clock over the entry pavilion was added in 1906.

Left: St. Louis City Hall is modeled on the 17th-century Hôtel de Ville in Paris

Top: The rotunda with its gold glass skylight was the last feature of the building to be completed

PATRICK HENRY SCHOOL

1230 North 10th Street
William Ittner
1906

During his 13-year tenure as Commissioner of School Buildings and an additional four-year stint as the school board's consulting architect, William Ittner transformed public education in the city by designing 50 new public school buildings. "The newer public school buildings of St. Louis are probably the best in the United States … The exterior appearance of the buildings could hardly be improved," noted a report by the United States Schoolhouse Commission in 1908 that singled out the Patrick Henry School as exemplifying the city's enlightened approach. The school's extraordinarily intricate brickwork – which combines Arts & Crafts, Moorish and other motifs – is one of the prolific Ittner's most impressive creations.

Left and Top: The Patrick Henry School's elaborate brickwork incorporates Moorish and Arts & Crafts motifs

ROBERTS, JOHNSON & RAND SHOE COMPANY BUILDING

Northwest corner of 15th Street and Washington Avenue
Theodore Link
1910

Eighteen years after the completion of the Wainwright Building, architect Theodore Link designed what is in most respects an exact replica. The differences are mainly cosmetic – gray limestone as opposed to Sullivan's brick and sandstone and eclectic ornamentation that combines Classical and Egyptian motifs instead of Sullivan's intensely personal naturalistic and geometric designs. (The Art Deco entrance on Washington Avenue was added in the 1930s.) The building served as offices for Roberts, Johnson & Rand, the largest footwear company in the city, which later morphed into the International Shoe Co. and, still later, Interco. In the late 1990s, the much-praised redevelopment of the complex into the City Museum by sculptors Robert and Gail Cassily was the beginning of a wide-ranging revitalization of the surrounding neighborhood.

MUNICIPAL COURTS BUILDING

1320 Market Street
Isaac Taylor
1911

One of architect Isaac Taylor's final commissions, the Municipal Courts Building demonstrates his thorough mastery of the Classical idiom after a 40-year career that began when he joined the office of George Barnett as an apprentice in 1868. The budget for the building was $2 million, which did not allow for a 150-foot tower that was part of the original design. The sculptural grouping over the Market Street entrance is by noted Neapolitan sculptor Vincenzo Alfano and depicts "Truth and Justice." Alfano also completed commissions for the 1904 World's Fair.

ST. LOUIS PUBLIC LIBRARY

Northeast corner of Olive and 13th streets
Cass Gilbert
1912

In 1907, the Washington University School of Architecture invited nine architecture firms – including such well-known local designers as Theodore Link and William Ittner – to participate in a competition for the purpose of selecting a design for St. Louis's new central library. The winner was Cass Gilbert, a New York architect already well known to St. Louis residents as the creator of the St. Louis Art Museum in Forest Park. Gilbert, one of the country's preeminent Classicists, proposed a two-story Italian Renaissance palazzo that is one of the city's most extraordinary structures. Gilbert's buildings are nothing if not literate and reflect his extensive knowledge of history and art. The granite façade includes 30 shields engraved with the names of 36 printers – starting with Gutenberg and ending with William Morris – who were leaders in early book publishing. The highlight of the interior is the two-story delivery room, which features bronze chandeliers, brass doorways, a gilded ceiling and a marble floor modeled on the Pantheon in Rome. Also notable are two reading rooms – the Art Room and the Periodical Room – modeled on well-known Florentine interiors, respectively, di Cambio's 13th-century Church of La Badia and Michelangelo's 16th-century Biblioteca Laurenziana. The building cost $1.5 million, $500,000 of which came from a grant from industrialist Andrew Carnegie. In 1928, local businessman George Fox Steedman funded the construction of the Steedman Architectural Library off the Art Room, a one-room addition not visible from the street, which was designed by Mauran, Russell & Crowell. The room houses Steedman's collection of rare architectural books.

Left: The St. Louis Public Library's delivery room features bronze chandeliers, brass doorways, a gilded ceiling and a marble floor modeled on the Pantheon in Rome

Top: The main lobby includes an elaborate vaulted ceiling

INTAKE TOWER #2

Mississippi River at Chain of Rocks Bridge
Roth & Study
1915

Guy Study – architect, critic, pioneering preservationist – was one of the more intriguing figures in the St. Louis architecture world in the early decades of the 20th century. Like Harvey Ellis, he was best at smaller commissions that demonstrated his impressive command of historically accurate Classical and Medieval styles. Intake Tower #2, which was built for the St. Louis water department and includes living quarters, embodies St. Louis architecture: a miniature Classical palace in the river. The limestone structure sits on a granite foundation that – in order to withstand the Mississippi's mighty flow – goes down 100 feet to bedrock.

MISSOURI ATHLETIC ASSOCIATION

MISSOURI ATHLETIC CLUB

405 Washington Avenue
William Ittner and George Brueggeman
1916

Heroically scaled and with one of the mightiest overhangs in the city, this brick and stone palazzo at the foot of the Eads Bridge has been the social and recreational heart of the downtown business elite for close to a century. The building is the Missouri Athletic Club's second home. The first – on the same site – burned in 1914, killing 37 people, still one of the city's worst fires. The current building – which cost $650,000 to construct and another $250,000 to furnish – is, in some ways, a reaction to that catastrophe. "The structure is (of) fireproof construction (with) the only wood used … being the wainscoting, doors and the gymnasium floor and the floor in the private banquet hall," noted the *St. Louis Post Dispatch* in a story that ran shortly before the building opened. The 10-story façade is divided into thirds that reflect the different functions within: dining and public rooms on the lower floors, gymnasium and natatorium in the middle and sleeping rooms and suites on top. The building is a tour de force of brickwork, particularly the upper floors where architect William Ittner's distinctive crosshatching reaches its apotheosis. Inside, the building retains much of its pre-war grandeur. The Club's eclectic art collection began in 1918 when a handful of members donated $25 apiece towards the purchase of *Windswept Meramec River*, a landscape by architect and painter Thomas Barnett.

SOUTHWESTERN BELL BUILDING

1010 Pine Street
Mauran, Russell & Crowell
1926

Skyscraper designers in the 1920s believed that building setbacks that allowed light and air to penetrate to the sidewalk were the best way to mitigate the "canyon effect" caused by rows of high rises in downtown commercial districts. The 33-story Southwestern Bell Building – which has setbacks at its 13th, 17th, 20th and 23rd floors – tests the validity of that theory with mostly felicitous results. The tower – which cost $8 million to construct – was the tallest structure in the city until the construction of the Gateway Arch in the 1960s. The building occupies a square block and the back, or south, side was left unfinished as it was designed to back up to a proposed addition that never materialized. What did materialize, however, was the Gateway Mall. In 1989, St. Louis-based Wedemeyer Cernick Corrubia completed a renovation that involved cladding the back in limestone that matched the other three sides and reorienting the building's main entrance to the mall.

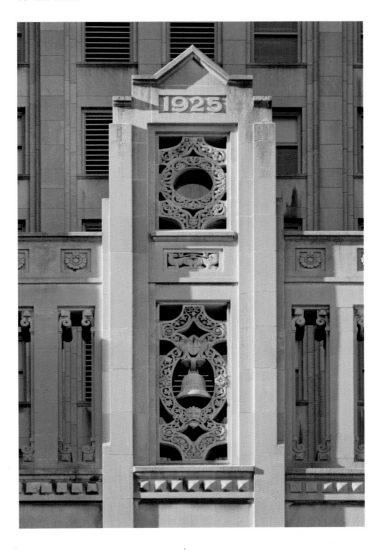

Far Left: The Southwestern Bell Building has setbacks on the 13th, 17th, 20th and 23rd floors

Left: The ornamentation over the original main entrance includes the telephone company's logo, a carved stone bell

CONTINENTAL BUILDING

3615 Olive Street
William Ittner
1929

Architect William Ittner's final large commission was unlike anything else in his oeuvre – a gleaming white terra cotta skyscraper that incorporates four large relief sculptures of Colonial figures in a façade bristling with Neo-Gothic details. The 22-story structure was completed on the eve of the Great Depression for an Arkansas financier named Edward Mays who planned to both live and work in the building. The lower floors were occupied by Mays' two companies, Continental Life Insurance and the Grand National Bank, while the top three floors were converted into what was in all probability the city's only triplex penthouse. Mays went bankrupt shortly afterwards and the building reverted to being a general office tower whose tenants over the years have included General Motors, Dow Chemical and David O. Selznick Movie Studios.
The neighborhood went into steep decline in the 1960s and the building's last tenant moved out in 1973. After sitting vacant for over a quarter of a century, the building was renovated into residential units in the early 2000s.

FOX THEATER

525 North Grand Avenue
C. Howard Crane
1929

In the late 1920s, Detroit architect C. Howard Crane designed three delirious movie theaters for producer William Fox in St. Louis, Detroit and Brooklyn. The theaters all had similar interiors, which were described at the time as being in the "Siamese Byzantine" style, an evident euphemism for anything goes. The Fox cost $6 million to construct and another $700,000 to furnish and defies any rational architectural analysis. Best just to enjoy the 90-foot lobby's gilded ceiling and gigantic red and gold Corinthian columns, the 4,000-plus-seat auditorium with its elaborate "Louis this" and "Louis that" plaster details, the 2,700-pipe Wurlitzer organ, the leather-lined elevators and the two-and-a-half-ton pot metal chandelier that includes 2,264 pieces of colored glass and 259 light bulbs. The exterior, meanwhile, features some of the most exuberant terra cotta ornamentation in the city. Both the St. Louis and Detroit theaters have been restored and are now the cultural linchpins of their respective neighborhoods. The Brooklyn Fox, meanwhile, was demolished in 1971.

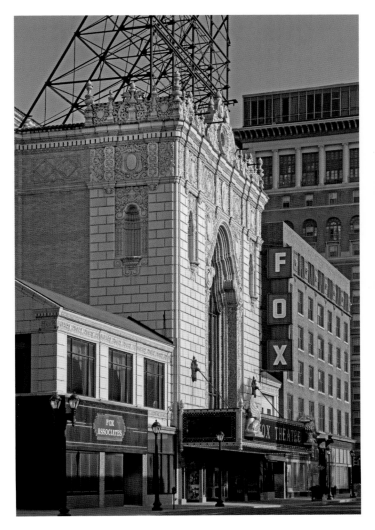

Far Left: The Fox Theater's proscenium is crowned by a gilded elephant's head

Left: The richly colored "Siamese Byzantine" auditorium

83

CIVIL COURTS BUILDING

Bounded by Tucker Boulevard, 11th, Market and Chestnut streets
Klipstein & Rathmann
1930

"A new temple of justice has been erected," said Missouri Governor Henry Caulfield – apparently without irony – at the opening of the Civil Courts Building. The 14-story building is topped by a two-story Greek temple, a stepped Egyptian pyramid and two enormous aluminum griffins – or are they sphinxes? No one seems quite sure. The model was one of the seven wonders of the ancient world – the Mausoleum of Halicarnassus, a tomb built for King Mausolus in 353 BC in what is now Turkey. For all the theatrics, there is symbolic logic to the building: the workaday lower floors contain chambers and courtrooms while the Greek temple is occupied by an airy law library where, presumably, judges research and meditate on their decisions. The griffins, meanwhile, were the most discussed feature of the building. Some claimed they represented watchfulness and guardianship, others righteousness and mercy. What is indisputable is that they also serve a less exalted function as lightening rods.

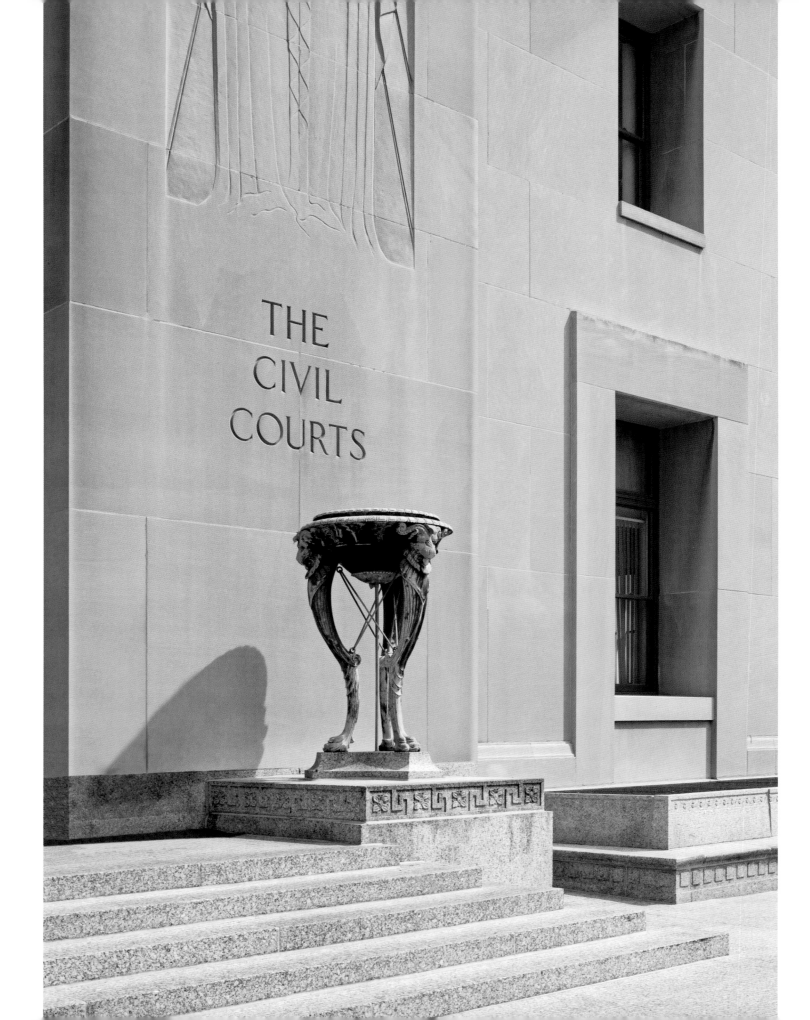

THE
CIVIL
COURTS

Far Left: The Civil Courts Building's main entrance is framed by delicate bronze urns

Left: The deeply recessed windows give the building weight and definition

TUMS BUILDING

313 4th Street
Widmer Engineers (Arthur J. Widmer)
1933

As in many cities, St. Louis's first exposure to the Bauhaus came via the industrial sector. This five-story terra cotta and concrete building – constructed for and still occupied by the manufacturer of a popular digestive aid – was designed by Arthur J. Widmer, a 1904 graduate of Cornell University's Mechanical Engineering School, who moved to St. Louis in 1907. Over the course of his long career, he designed over a thousand bridges, grain elevators, hospitals and industrial buildings. A trade magazine advertisement of the period conveys Widmer's functionalist approach: "Widmer Engineers (will) make a complete survey, lay out your plan, draw the plans and do all engineering and construction work. You get a better building in less time. You save money by escaping the compounded fees and charges of architects, engineers, general contractors and sub-contractors."

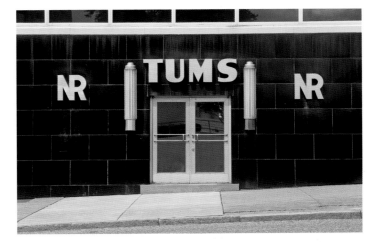

JEWEL BOX

Forest Park
William C.E. Becker
1936

The Jewel Box marked a turning point in St. Louis's civic architecture. In a park noted for its many classically inspired structures, city engineer William C.E. Becker took his design cues from such modern sources as the airplane hangar and the long, low industrial buildings of Detroit architect Albert Kahn. The surprise is how well this fundamentally utilitarian style works for buildings of an ornamental and ceremonial nature. The clearly visible skeleton-like steel structure – a hallmark of the Bauhaus but also highly characteristic of such Victorian icons as London's Crystal Palace – has a delicate beauty not unlike that of the flowers and plants the building shelters. The total cost was $117,000, about half of which was WPA (Works Progress Administration) stimulus money from the Federal government.

GRANT CLINIC

114 North Taylor Street
Harris Armstrong
1938

This commission by architect Harris Armstrong – a compact brick medical office for Dr. Samuel B. Grant that recalls both Frank Lloyd Wright (the large windows and roof overhang) and Eliel Saarinen (the brick and copper details) – was strongly predictive of the direction Modernism would take in St. Louis.

MILLES FOUNTAIN

Aloe Plaza between 18th and 20th streets
Carl Milles
1940

"The strangest wedding in America was celebrated last month in front of Union Station in St. Louis," reported *Life Magazine* in June of 1940 about the unveiling of what was then known as "The Wedding of the Waters." The fountain, which consists of 19 mythological bronze figures frolicking in a stone basin, symbolizes the nearby confluence of the Mississippi and Missouri Rivers. The male figure and his retinue of tritons represent the former while the female figure and her mermaid attendants symbolize the latter. The fountain got off to a rocky start when it was widely denounced in the press as obscene. The eventual solution was to downplay the wedding aspect by renaming it "The Meeting of the Waters." Milles's response to the controversy was playful: "To you boys and girls in the pool," he said at the unveiling, "Behave well, enjoy life, but remember that at every sunrise you have to be here." Today, it is widely known as Milles Fountain. Milles was the first in a long line of artists and architects with connections to Eliel Saarinen's Cranbrook Academy of Art outside of Detroit to execute substantial commissions in St. Louis.

96

96

Left and Top: Milles Fountain features
19 mythological bronze figures
frolicking in a stone basin

LAMBERT FIELD MAIN TERMINAL

10701 Natural Bridge Road
Hellmuth, Yamasaki & Leinweber (Minoru Yamasaki)
1955

In the early 1950s, Minoru Yamasaki toured a number of recently built air terminals around the country in search of ideas for the new Main Terminal at Lambert Field. "All were disappointing," he recalled. The answer, he decided, was to go back to the future. "My memories of the great space at Grand Central Station in New York offered a much better example," he said. The highlight of Yamasaki's three-story design is the top-floor ticketing and waiting area – a series of three supremely elegant halls with 32-foot barrel-vaulted ceilings constructed of thin-shell concrete. The halls echo one of Classicism's most durable models, the Roman Baths of Caracalla, while at the same time establishing a new template for the jet age. A fourth hall was added in 1965. When it opened, the western hall contained a restaurant separated from the nearby waiting area by an elaborate metal screen by noted artist Harry Bertoia. The screen, which was 48 feet long and 8 feet tall, was removed and evidently sold for scrap during a subsequent renovation. A model of the screen is in the St. Louis Art Museum.

STEINBERG HALL

Washington University
Fumihiko Maki
1960

In 1958, Fumihiko Maki, then a 30-year-old associate in Washington University's campus planning office, was asked to design a new building containing a library, auditorium and gallery for the University's art and architecture schools. "Everything was more informal in that era," Maki says today. "I had students build the model (and) I did all the perspectives and drawings myself." The resulting two-story structure – his first commission as an architect – is a playful exercise in "folded plate" concrete construction with a delicate – and much-imitated – crinkle-cut roof and portico.

CLIMATRON

Missouri Botanical Garden
Murphy & Mackey
1960

Years before Buckminster Fuller's geodesic dome captured the world's imagination at Montreal's Expo '67 World's Fair, architects Joseph Murphy and Eugene Mackey employed similar principles and technology to design the world's first climate-controlled greenhouse at the Missouri Botanical Garden. The dome, which is 70 feet tall and 175 feet in diameter, has no interior columns – the weight, rather, is distributed throughout the structure via interlocking aluminum rods. A two-year renovation in the late 1980s involved replacing the original Plexiglass panels with heat-tempered glass. The structure houses over 2,800 plants in a computer-controlled rainforest environment. In 1976, the American Institute of Architects named the Climatron one of the 100 most significant architectural achievements in United States history.

JAMES S. MCDONNELL PLANETARIUM

Forest Park
Hellmuth, Obata & Kassabaum (Gyo Obata)
1963

The form is based on a hyperboloid, a mathematical theorem relating to the curvature of lines – pure abstraction, in other words. Standing in front of it, however, the associations are more literal – a Mid-Century lampshade? Audrey Hepburn's Givenchy hat? The McDonnell Planetarium may be the kickiest 1960s building in the city. It's both massive and delicate simultaneously – the enormous curved concrete shell is only 3 inches thick. At night, the exterior lighting makes the structure glow like an alabaster lamp. Inside is the Starbridge, a domed space where various views of the nighttime sky are projected onto the ceiling. The building also includes a café and gift shop. A staircase winds around the dome to a rooftop observation deck.

GATEWAY ARCH

Downtown Riverfront
Eero Saarinen & Associates
1965

The Arch symbolizes St. Louis in the same way the Statue of Liberty does New York and the Eiffel Tower stands for Paris. It is, without question, the most famous structure in the city. It also happens to be a masterpiece. This is fortunate, because its construction involved one of the more wrenching trade-offs in architectural history – that being the sacrifice of the Levee District, a 40-block area along the river that at one time was the largest cast-iron neighborhood west of New York's Soho. The Arch, which honors St. Louis's role in the westward expansion of the United States, began with a competition in 1948 that attracted such entrants as Walter Gropius, Louis Kahn, Eliel Saarinen and Skidmore Owings & Merrill. The surprise winner was Eliel's son, 38-year-old Eero Saarinen, who proposed a 630-foot-tall catenary arch executed in stainless steel. Due to funding issues, the project – which also included extensive landscaping by noted landscape architect Dan Kiley – did not begin construction until 1959. Saarinen himself did not live to see the completion of what is generally considered his greatest design. He died in 1961 at the age of 51.

AMERICAN ZINC, LEAD & SMELTING COMPANY BUILDING

20 South 4th Street
Hellmuth, Obata & Kassabaum (Gyo Obata)
1967

The American Zinc Building is "one of the simplest ... office buildings"
as well as "one of the clearest expressions of any structural system I have
designed," said Gyo Obata of the four-story, 30,000-square-foot stainless
steel structure he created for a leading metals producer. The structural system
is a Vierendeel truss, a steel bridge truss invented in the 1890s by Belgian
engineer Arthur Vierendeel. Using the truss as an architectural element allowed
for column-free floors as well as rows of large windows on the upper stories.
The stainless steel cladding reflects both the tenant as well as the nearby
Gateway Arch.

PET PLAZA

400 South 4th Street
A.L. Aydelott
1969

A.L. Aydelott, a Memphis architect, carved out an interesting career in the 1950s and 60s as a designer of Brutalist structures with Pet Plaza being his most significant commission. Brutalism, a 1960s offshoot of Modernism, is characterized by massive, unadorned, concrete forms that clearly reflect their interior uses. The 15-story Pet building – designed as offices for a food and beverage company – consists of a two-story glass lobby, nine column-free floors of office space, a balconied conference center and a top floor executive wing. Unusual for its time, the building contained numerous custom-designed fixtures. The total cost was $11 million, making it one of the city's more expensive 1960s office buildings. In 2006, the building was converted to residential apartments. Aydelott also designed a residence in suburban Ladue built for Pet's chairman and president, Theodore Gamble.

GENERAL AMERICAN LIFE BUILDING

Market, Walnut, 7th and 8th streets
Philip Johnson and John Burgee
1977

In what now seems like the glide path for Post-Modernism, there was a period in the late 1970s when architects were fascinated by the possibilities of basic geometric forms such as squares, triangles and circles. New York architect Philip Johnson, always attuned to shifts in design, explored this trend in his only St. Louis commission, the General American Life Building. Built as the home office for an insurance company, the 150,000-square-foot structure consists of two three-story triangular wings separated by a six-story glass cylinder, with one of the wings elevated 45 feet on a forest of steel columns in order to create an imposing entrance. Inside, the cylinder contains an elevator bank and service core. Johnson described the building as a "square doughnut with a round hole," and noted that, "We have triangles, squares, circles, cylinders, all this geometry expressed in this one building."

1010 MARKET

1010 Market Street
Edward Larrabee Barnes
1981

"I've always been drawn to making things as simple as possible, if you can do that without making them inhuman or dull or oppressive," said New York architect Edward Larrabee Barnes about his design philosophy. His proposal for 1010 Market, a 20-story speculative office tower plus a smaller four-story building intended as the new home for a local television station, fulfills this credo. The granite tower features a notched corner that transforms the building into an enormous folding screen. The notching also significantly increases the number of corner offices inside. The tower is connected to the smaller building by a two-story covered passageway that has the feel of a triumphal arch.

Top: One AT&T Center is partially
modeled on the 1926 Southwestern
Bell Building across the street

ONE AT&T CENTER

900 Pine Street
Hellmuth, Obata & Kassabaum (Gyo Obata)
1986

This 44-story office tower – the tallest building in Missouri
when it was completed – is the product of an interesting
moment in late-20th-century architecture when designers
briefly rebelled against the strictures of Modernism and
reverted to pre-war models. "As you know, there has been
a reaction in recent years against buildings that are plain and
straight sided," said architect Gyo Obata at the time. "I (wanted)
to give the Bell building a stronger presence but not with a
Beaux Arts model in mind. I was thinking more of the earlier
skyscrapers like the RCA Building in New York and the old
Southwestern Bell Building on the block just west." For
all the exterior pre-war trappings, the interior is decidedly
high-tech. The $120 million project includes 16 miles of
fiber optic cable connected to 1,500 computer terminals.

PULITZER FOUNDATION FOR THE ARTS

3716 Washington Avenue
Tadao Ando
2001

This building – a private museum that houses the superb
Modern art collection assembled by Emily Rauh Pulitzer and
her late husband, publishing heir Joseph Pulitzer Jr. – was
Japanese architect Tadao Ando's first public commission in the
United States. The U-shaped concrete structure consists of
two parallel galleries separated by an outdoor reflecting pool.
The building has "wonderful walls," says Ellsworth Kelly,
one of two artists – the other is Richard Serra – who were
commissioned to create individual works of art for the museum.
Kelly's piece, "Blue Black," a 28-foot two-panel work, occupies
the larger of the two galleries, a two-story rectangular space.
A broad flight of stairs ascends to a terrace that looks out
on beds of waving prairie grass and a side yard containing
Serra's "Joe", a coiled Corten steel maze named for Ms.
Pulitzer's late husband. "Even in a raw urban site," said Ando,
"I wanted to create a space for the contemplation of art and
the cultivation of spirit."

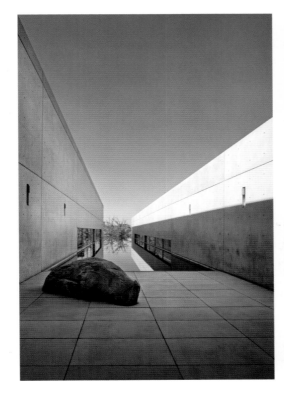

Left: The Pulitzer Foundation for the Arts' staircase leads to a rooftop terrace

Top: The building's two wings frame an infinity pool

Top right: The windows of Emily Rauh Pulitzer's office look out on Richard Serra's "Joe," named for her late husband, Joseph Pulitzer Jr.

Right: The building's side yard

MILDRED LANE KEMPER
ART MUSEUM

Washington University
Fumihiko Maki
2006

Nearly half a century separates architect Fumihiko Maki's
two St. Louis commissions, Steinberg Hall and the Mildred
Lane Kemper Art Museum. Steinberg featured an innovative
folded plate concrete roof and was considered an experimental
building for its time. The Kemper, however, is a more
utilitarian structure. It is often said that Modernism is about
problem solving. The Kemper represents a successful solution
to challenging problems. The two-story 65,000-square-foot
building – which is located steps away from Steinberg – has
an unusually complicated program. In addition to galleries for
Washington University's extensive art collection, the building
contains offices, classrooms and a library for the University's
Sam Fox School of Design & Visual Arts. The grace notes
include a series of sculptural rooftop skylights as well as an
unornamented limestone façade that harmonizes with
Steinberg Hall.

CENTENE PLAZA

7700 Forsyth Boulevard
Clayton
Hellmuth Obata & Kassabaum (Gyo Obata)
2010

Built as the headquarters for a major healthcare services firm, Centene Plaza is the first new high-rise office tower to be erected in the St. Louis area in many years. The 17-story structure shows Gyo Obata – who has experimented with a number of architectural styles over the course of his 60-plus year career – adapting to the current vogue for ultra-transparent sustainable design. The structure has a diaphanous quality – its fritted glass façade and virtual cornice are simultaneously there but not there. The razor sharp corners, meanwhile, are almost Gothic in their severity. Another highlight is the building's plaza, which features a spectacular covered walkway with a colored glass canopy by British artist Liam Gillick. The building – which includes a number of energy-saving features – is expected to have a Gold LEED rating from the U.S. Green Building Council.

ELLEN S. CLARK HOPE PLAZA AT BJC INSTITUTE OF HEALTH

Euclid Avenue and Children's Place
Maya Lin with Michael Van Valkenburgh Associates
2010

Maya Lin, the creator of the Vietnam War Memorial in Washington, D.C., as well as numerous other highly acclaimed works, designed this ethereal memorial to civic activist and longtime Barnes-Jewish Hospital supporter Ellen S. Clark, who died in March of 2010. The highlight is a circular lily pond 80 feet in diameter with a disappearing edge that suggests infinity. A smaller circular viewing platform extends over the pond and is fritted with LED lights. The lights recreate the night sky on Christmas Day 1959, which was Mrs. Clark's birthday. The surrounding 2.2-acre plaza is planted with dozens of redbud, willow, white oak and Kentucky coffee trees as well as grasses and other native plants.

Index of Buildings

Index of Architects, Architecture Firms, Designers and Artists

Bibliography

Benson, Sally. *Meet Me In St. Louis*. New York:
Random House, 1941

Bryan, John Albury. *Missouri's Contribution to American Architecture*.
St. Louis: St. Louis Architectural Club, 1928

Cronon, William. *Nature's Metropolis: Chicago and the Great West*.
New York: W.W. Norton & Company, 1991

Faherty, William Barnaby. *Henry Shaw: His Life and Legacies*.
St. Louis: Missouri Botanical Garden Press, 2001

Faherty, William Barnaby, and NiNi Harris. *St. Louis: A Concise
History*. St. Louis: St. Stanislaus Historical Museum Society, 2004

Hallenberg, Heather M. *Form, Function, Fusion: The Architecture of
Isaac S. Taylor 1850–1917*. Master of Arts Thesis. Columbia:
University of Missouri, 1979

Lowic, Lawrence. *The Architectural Heritage of St. Louis 1803–1891*.
St. Louis: Washington University Gallery of Art, 1982

McCue, George, and Frank Peters. *A Guide to the Architecture of
St. Louis*. Columbia: University of Missouri Press, 1989

Moore, Robert J. *The Gateway Arch: An Architectural Dream*.
St. Louis: Jefferson National Parks Association, 2005

Morrison, Hugh. *Louis Sullivan: Prophet of Modern Architecture*.
New York: W.W. Norton & Company, 1935

Mumford, Eric (editor). *Modern Architecture in St. Louis: Washington
University and Postwar American Architecture 1948–1973*. St. Louis:
Washington University School of Architecture, 2004

Norris, Amy S. *Missouri Athletic Club: 100 Years of Excellence*.
St. Louis: Missouri Athletic Club, 2002

O'Gorman, James F. *Three American Architects: Richardson, Sullivan and
Wright 1865–1915*. Chicago: University of Chicago Press, 1992

Oelsen, Laure. *George I. Barnett 1815–1898*. Master of Arts Thesis.
Columbia: University of Missouri, 1973

Petroski, Henry. *Engineers of Dreams*. New York:
Alfred A. Knopf, 1995

Primm, James Neal. *Lion of the Valley: St. Louis Missouri 1764–1980*.
St. Louis: Missouri Historical Society press, 1981

Reps, John W. *Cities of the Mississippi: Nineteenth Century Images of
Urban Development*. Columbia: University of Missouri Press, 1994

Sandweiss, Lee Ann (editor). *Seeking St. Louis: Voices from
a River City 1670–2000*. St. Louis: Missouri Historical Society
Press, 2000

Toft, Carolyn Hewes, and Lynn Josse. *St. Louis: Landmarks &
Historic Districts*. St. Louis: Landmarks Association of
St. Louis, 2002

Toft, Carolyn Hewes, and Osmund Overby. *Laclede's Landing:
A History and Architectural Guide*. St. Louis: Landmarks Association
of St. Louis, 1977

Twain, Mark. *Life on the Mississippi*. Mineola, New York:
Dover Publications, 2000

Yamasaki, Minoru. *A Life in Architecture*. New York:
John Weatherhill, 1979